America's
Oak Furnitu

Nancy N. Schiffer

Photographs by Christopher Biondi

Revised Price Guide

Schiffer Publishing Ltd

4880 Lower Valley Rd. Atglen, PA 19310 USA

Acknowledgments

The many people who contributed their knowledge, time and examples of American oak furniture to this project are appreciated deeply. Building upon past experience has brought us to this level of recognition, and it is assumed that the knowledge will continue to build as interest is focused on the subject. The author thanks Chris Biondi and Bob Biondi for their art of photography; Sharon and Lou Daniels of Oak House Antiques, Patascala, Ohio; Eileen and Richard Dubrow of Dubrow Antiques, Bayside, Long Island, New York; Francis (Pidge) Polito of Polito Antiques, West Chester, Pennsylvania; Steve, Norb and Nancy Reidle of Southwood Antiques, Dallastown, Pennsylvania; and Rob Stevens and Carol Lehman of Stevens Antiques, Frazer, Pennsylvania.

Since the publication of America's Oak Furniture in 1989, a group of very serious Oak Collectors from across our Nation have become involved in pursuing the "Cream of the Oak". These intense Oak Collectors are major players in the Antique Oak World. Distance does not slow them...as communication, transportation and shipping are readily available.

When special items are released from current collections, these Major Oak Buyers are well aware of it. They know all and they will be ready.

The fair sale is at Auction and auctions bearing such "fruit" are well advertised. The competition is fierce, and rightly so, as the availability of these items is very limited. The prices soar. A current value is established.

Many of the sought after Oak Pieces are included in America's Oak Furniture. Several of these exact pieces, owned at first publication, have recently been sold and have become part of the new accumulating collections across our country. (i.e., the Hall Seat containing the Clock/Canopied China Closet.)

The value of quality American Oak Furniture has greatly increased in the past decade. Ten percent to twenty percent per year is a good average although many specific items have more than doubled their value.

The only value the Oak knows...is UP!

Velma Warren
Price Guide 1998

Front cover:
Small desk—see 68C
Large desk—see 68A
Chair—see 13D

Back cover:
Wardrobe—see 112C
Chair—see 12D

Title page
Hat and coat rack of turned elements with five turned legs. *$375*. Roll top desk of unusual large size and interesting fitted interior. *$10,000*

Revised price guide: 1998
Copyright © 1988 by Nancy N. Schiffer.
Library of Congress Catalog Card Number: 88-64078.

ISBN: 0-7643-0580-8
Printed in United States of America
1 2 3 4

Published by Schiffer Publishing Ltd.
4880 Lower Valley Road
Atglen, PA 19310
Phone: (610) 593-1777; Fax: (610) 593-2002
E-mail: Schifferbk@aol.com
Please write for a free catalog.
This book may be purchased from the publisher.
Please include $3.95 for shipping.

In Europe, Schiffer books are distributed by
Bushwood Books
6 Marksbury Avenue
Kew Gardens
Surrey TW9 4JF England
Phone: 44 (0)181 392-8585; Fax: 44 (0)181 392-9876
E-mail: Bushwd@aol.com

Please try your bookstore first.
We are interested in hearing from authors
with book ideas on related subjects.

Contents

Combination fall front desk and book-case by the Larkin Co., Buffalo, New York. *$2500.*

Center table of oak with oval top and skirt, scrolled supports and platform base on scrolled feet. *$650.*

Sideboard with beveled mirror back, serpentine case and cabriole legs ending in scroll feet. *$1500.*

Large roll top desk with small drawers and shelves on the interior. The two side cases each contain three drawers. Shown with roll top closed at 69A. *$4500.*

Preface

The American, machine-made oak furniture shown in this book reflects improved mechanical technology which enabled prices of furniture to come within range for a middle-income family. They could purchase styles for their home that up to then they could have only dreamt about. The furniture will be seen to be a part of the culture in which it was made and used.

As the nineteenth century progressed and the economic structure of America grew, entrepreneurs found it efficient to join with others to form consolidated businesses and corporations. Middle-level managers evolved between the workmen and the owners. These managers formed the growing middle class who wanted all the comforts that only the upper class formerly could afford. As the businesses grew and became more efficient, improved machinery and mass production brought prices down to levels this middle class could afford.

As the products became more affordable, the demand for them increased, and therefore production increased. With expanded production, new markets needed to be developed. Improving transportation systems, such as railroads and better highways reduced shipping costs which made possible the distribution of furniture throughout the country.

For example, in Grand Rapids, Michigan, the first furniture factory was built by Robert Hilson and Sylvester Granger in 1836. Mr. Hilson opened the first chair factory there in 1837. By 1890, there were 38 factories in Grand Rapids because there they had an unlimited supply of hard woods. The Grand Rapids and Indiana Railroad extended the entire length of the state through the hardwood territory.

The human resources in the growing mid-west of America included German and Scandinavian immigrants skilled in woodworking techniques, and they helped determine the styles which became popular there, too. In Grand Rapids, for example, the population in 1850 was 3,000 people. By 1870, it was 16,000 people. In 1880, 32,000 people, and in 1884, the population was 42,000 people. It is no wonder, then, that American development is seen in a microcosm in the furniture industry.

The rapid increase in inventions during the nineteenth century is illustrated most dramatically by records at the U. S. Patent Office in Washington, D.C. From 1790 to 1840, 12,421 patents were issued in the United States. On April 10, 1890, Patent number 425,395 was issued. This country was bursting with innovation to match its growth in population.

As American businesses grew, commercial offices became needed, and the furniture industry saw an opportunity for new forms of furniture specialized for more efficient work places. Desks in many styles including the roll top were invented, filing drawers, office chairs, and work tables were designed.

As the decades advanced during this period, the workday became limited to ten or nine hours, creating more leisure time at home. With these changes evolved furniture forms to accommodate leisure time: rocking chairs, reclining chairs, and upholstered furniture.

The oak furniture shown on the following pages represents forms sold in local stores throughout the United States and available nationally through mail-order catalogs. Traveling salesmen represented one or more manufacturers. Many firms developed branches and regional sales offices in widespread cities.

Popular magazines provided written articles and advertising to broadcast new styles. Trade magazines brought news to the manufacturers of new machinery being patented and of his competition's advances. Trade associations brought manufacturers news of legislation, tariffs and union developments.

The mechanization in factories did not eclipse foot-powered machines in small factories and homes, for in the 1890's, advertisements for foot-powered machines were still carried in trade magazines.

In New England, as well as the Mid-West, towns developed around these factories. For the workers, the progress could be measured not so much in their increased paycheck as in the lower cost of goods which enabled their living standard to rise.

New furniture often could be purchased finished or unfinished, assembled or unassembled, and with or without hardware. Therefore, the examples shown in this book will have a variety of finished appearances, for in many ways they were individualized beyond their manufactured origins.

The finishes on oak furniture from this period are subjects of individual preference, both originally and through time as subsequent owners have "refinished" the furniture. The following eight different finishes for oak furniture are itemized in the Furniture Dealer's Reference Book of 1928, and can be taken to represent close to the styles popular in the decades preceding. The colors are arranged from lighter to darker shades:

SILVER GRAY OAK—White tones, yellow overall. This is a water stain which after it has dried and has been sanded, is filled with a thin white filler, then shellaced and waxed.

OFFICE OAK—Light yellow. Natural oak finish produced with filler only, the quality of the finish depending upon the wood and the way the filler is packed int the pores. Usually finished in varnish or shellac.

GOLDEN OAK—Golden tones, dark in the recesses. Usually made by thinning an antique filler to such a degree as to produce the desired shade. Finished in shellac and varnish, rubbed dull.

POLLARD OAK—Light brown. This is a two stain operation. The ground color is made with water stain and the shading is done with an oil stain. Usually produced in shades according to the designs and styles of furniture. Finished in wax.

FUMED OAK—Medium brown. Open pore finish made either by fuming or staining. Staining should be done with water stain. Usually finished in wax over shellac. The best finishes are made with wax over wood lacquer.

SPANISH OAK—Medium brown, gold tones. A water stain highlighted with sand paper or steel wool. Often decorated with painted sections and finished with wood lacquer.

ITALIAN OAK—Dark brown. Water stain applied after the wood has been sponged. The original medium brown tone can be darkened by applying a second coat. It is an open pore, wax finished.

EARLY ENGLISH OAK—An old favorite produced with an oil stain or a water stain and usually finished dull; either shellac, varnish or wood lacquer, rubbed dull.

Hardware is not stressed in the examples in this book because so many pieces lack "original" hardware, and the variety to choose from has always been an individual matter. As the furniture industry developed, specialized support businesses grew. Firms which made only the hardware, carved ornaments, veneers, inlays and wheels filled orders for many furniture manufacturers. Therefore, identification of a maker by these details is impossible.

In this book, mention of a maker is made only when it can be supported by a permanent label or mark. The manufacturers' catalog illustrations at the back of the book are presented with the manufacturer's identity intact.

References
Eileen and Richard Dubrow, *Furniture Made in America,* 1875-1905, Exton, Pennsylvania, 1982.

The Furniture Dealer's Reference Book, 1928, new reprint edition as *American Manufactured Furniture,* Schiffer Publishing, West Chester, Pennsylvania, 1988.

Chairs

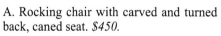

A. Rocking chair with carved and turned back, caned seat. *$450.*

B. Slat-back rocking chair with upholstered seat. *$250.*

C. Rocking chair with carved crest and seven splats, solid seat. *$300.*

D. Rocking chair with carved crest and six splats. *$275.*

E. Dished slat-back rocking chair with carving, scrolled knuckles and solid seat. *$350.*

F. Sleigh style rocking chair with upholstered back and seat. (Sold in 1998 at Auction). *$1100.*

A. Platform rocking chair with seven splats and solid seat. (Glider). *$750.*

B. Platform rocking chair with twist-turned stiles and upholstered back and seat. (George Hunzinger Design). *$1750.*

C. Child's painted wicker rocking chair with cushion seat. *$350.*

D. Child's rocking chair with turnings, woven vine back and caned seat. *$300.*

E. Slat-back rocking chair with carving and turnings, caned seat. *$500.*

F. Rocking chair with leather upholstery. *$275.*

WAREHOUSE, 23, 25, 27 AND 29 ELIZABETH STREET, CORNER CANAL STREET.
Dimensions, 50 x 150 feet.

FACTORY, 160 162. 164 AND 166 MONROE STREET, NEAR CLINTON STREET.
Dimensions, 100 x 100 feet.

Stickley-Brandt Furniture Co.

The Great Mail Order House

The factory and warehouse (top) and scenes from the manufacturing processes (right) of the M. & H. Schrenkeisen company in New York City where a wide range of furniture was made in 1885.

Advertising by furniture manufacturers helped to popularize new forms. This ad from a 1902 catalog of the Stickley-Brandt Furniture Company of Binghamton, New York confirms the widespread use of the mail service to solicit orders directly from consumers.

FACTORY OF M. & H. SCHRENKEISEN, NEW YORK CITY.

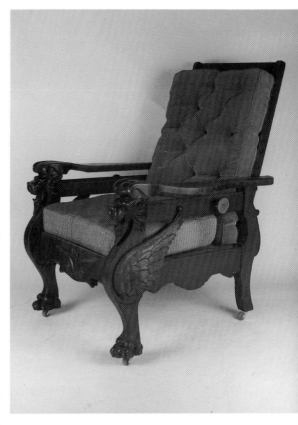

Opposite page:
A. Reclining chair with back and seat cushions. *$350.*

B. Reclining chair of horsechair upholstered back and seat in carved and turned frame. *$650.*

C. Reclining chair with upholstered back and cushion seat in solid frame. *$400.*

D. Reclining chair with cushion back and seat in frame carved with caryatid figures and scrolled feet; frame shown on the back cover. Exceptional. *$2800.*

A. Leather upholstered arm chair with carved wings. *$475.*

B. Carved arm chair with upholstered back and seat. *$1200.*

C. Reclining chair with cushion back and seat, and griffins carved into front legs. Unusual construction. *$1500.*

D. Carved arm chair with upholstered back, arm rests and seat, and griffins carved into the front supports. *$1500.*

Solid Construction and Solid Comfort in These Rockers

$2.85

NO. 72—This strikingly artistic rocking-chair has a panel of quartered oak and the entire chair is of solid oak, specially selected for its clear, smooth grain and beautiful figuring. The top is ornamented with carving in a tasteful design, and the legs, stretchers and posts are turned in a pleasing pattern. Price_____**$2.85**

$300

$4.35

NO. 55 W—Wood-seat Rocker made of quartered white oak and birch in mahogany finish; oak finished in the golden color, nicely polished. Height of back from seat, 21 inches. A handsome and serviceable chair at small cost. Price _____**$4.35**

$175

$3.50

NO. 51—Large arm Rocker, put together to sta The seat is covered with dark green leatherett and headrest upholstered and covered in leath erette with metal nails to match. May be ha in either golden oak or mahogany finis Price _____**$3.5C**

$200

$4.85

NO. 1160—This Rocker is designed specially for comfort, having a high back with a gently rounded formation of the cross panels and head rest, deep spring upholstered seat and wide arms. Quartered golden oak, highly polished. Seat is covered in figured Verona Velours___**$4.85**

$275

$4.35

NO. 2830—Large arm Rocker, modified mission design; extremely strong, well made and in every way serviceable. Quartered golden oak, selected figuring, finished golden. Broad shaped saddle seat, wide arm rests. Price___**$4.35**

$175

$9.65

NO. 534—High-Back Rocker made of quar tered white oak, golden finish, polished; als made in birch, veneered in genuine mahogany Spring seat upholstered in genuine leather panne plush. Price _____**$9.65**

$200

A Full Line of Arts and Crafts and Other Mission Furniture

Two pages from the S. Rosenbloom & Sons retail store catalog of 1909, from Syracuse, New York. The manufacturers are not identified in this catalog.

$33.00

No. 700 Rocker, **700A** Chair and **707** Settee—Mission Suite of three pieces, made of quartered white oak finished in the soft brown mission or weathered oak color; cushion made of genuine leather; simple, rich design. The settee is 45 inches long and 36 inches high, the chair and rocker are full size, 19 inches wide inside of arms. Remarkable value at

--**$33.00**

Settee----------**$16.50** | Rocker ----------------**$8.50** | Arm Chair------------**$8.00**

$250 $150, set $95

A. Child's arm chair with turned back supports and concave seat. *$225.*

B. Arm chair with deep carved slat and concave seat. *$300.*

C. Arm chair with pierced and carved back, lion head arms, concave seat and paw feet. *$1400.*

A. Child's high chair with turned back supports and solid seat. *$475.*

B. Windsor bow-back arm chair with carved knuckles and turned legs. Set of 6. *$1200.*

C. Arm chair with carved crest, thirteen turned spindles, and solid seat. *$350.*

D. Arm chair with carved crest, seven splats, bentwood arms and solid seat. *$500.*

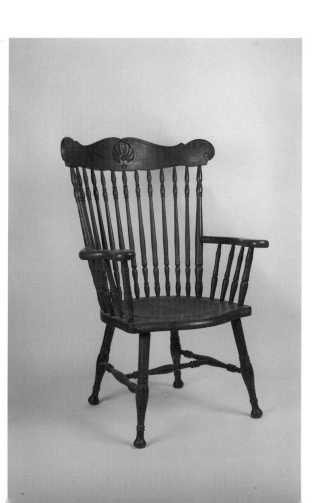

A. Desk chair with face design carved into the crest, seven back spindles, and pressed board seat. *$900.*

B. Desk chair with carved crest, seven splats and caned seat. *$700.*

C. Desk chair with carved crest, seven back splats and solid seat. *$650.*

A. Plain slat back desk chair with caned seat. *$350.*

B. Desk chair with carved crest monogrammed C C O, and leather upholstered back, arm rests and seat. *$2500.*

Opposite page:

A. Side chair with pierced lyre splat and solid seat. Set of 6. *$900.*

B. Side chair with pierced lyre shaped back and crest and flaring seat on turned legs. (Decorative) *$175.*

C. Side chair with solid urn splat and upholstered seat. (Ordinary) *$125.*

D. Side chair with solid urn splat and solid seat. Set of 6. *$900.*

A. Matching side and arm chairs with solid urn splats and upholstered seats. Set of 6 including 2 armchairs. *$1200.*

B. Side chair with carved deep crest and splat, two turned spindles and solid seat. *$250.*

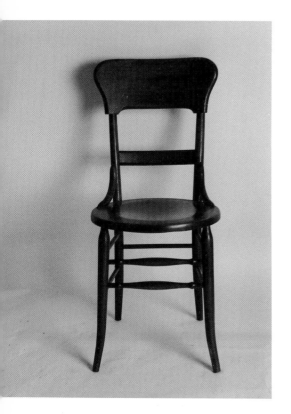

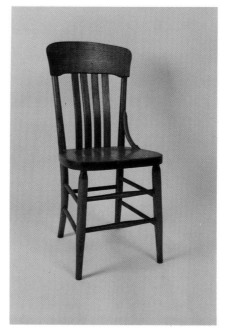

Opposite page:
A. Side chair with deep crest and slat, round solid seat. Set of 6. *$600.*

B. Child's side chair with four splats and rounded solid seat. *$125.*

C. Side chair with shaped crest and plain slat, solid seat and cabriole front legs. *$200.*

D. Matching arm and side chairs with four splats and solid seats on flared legs. Set of 6 with 2 arm-chairs. *$800.*

A. Chippendale style side chair with pierced splat, upholstered slip seat, cabriole legs and paw feet.*$550 for a single, sets of 8 to 10 are $700 each in sets.*

B. Side chair with plain crest and slat joined by seven spindles, caned seat. Set of 4. *$700.*

C. Side chair with carved crest, four spindles and caned seat. *$175 single.*

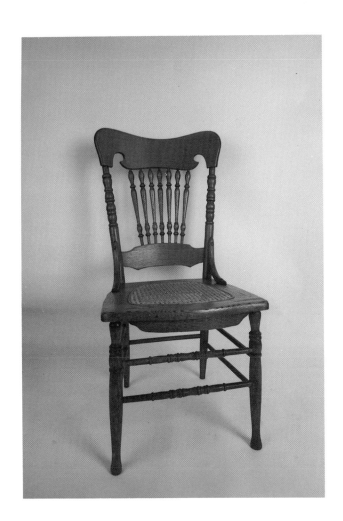

The Larkin Soap Company of Buffalo, New York offered furniture as premiums for points accumulated by selling Larkin soap products. The manufacturers of this furniture are not identified, and the recognized styles now carry the Larkin name. The four chairs shown on this page are known as four styles of Larkin chairs. They differ in their turnings, pressed decorative patterns and stretcher designs. Made in sets originally, they can be found as both side and arm chairs.

A. Larkin 1 side chair, set of 6-ea *$300.*

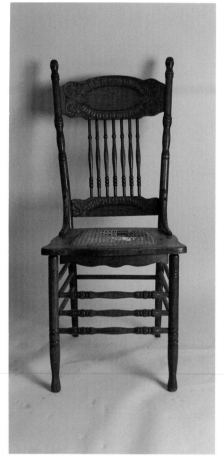

B. Larkin 2 side chair, set of 6-ea. *$275.*

C. Larkin 3 arm chair, *$500 as single, $600 ea. in pairs-$1200/pair.*

D. Larkin 4 side chair, *$250 ea. in set of 6.*

A. Side chair made by Haywood Wakefield with seven spiral turned spindles and pressed board seat. Set of 6-*$225 ea.*

B. Side chair with pressed slats and ten plain splats over a caned seat. Set of 6-*$200 ea.*

C. Side chair with pressed slats in a pattern which has become known as the North Wind design (enlargements at right show details). Seven turned spindles and a caned seat complete this design. Set of 6-*$275 ea.*

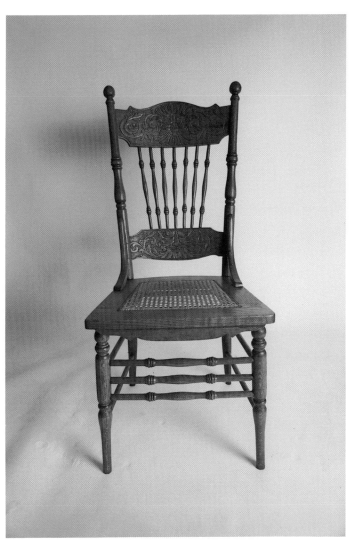

A. Side chair with pressed Stag's Head design in the crest (enlarged detail at right), eight turned spindles and a solid seat. *$375-set of 6-$2500.*

B. Side chair with carved and pierced crest, two plain slats, eleven turned spindles, and caned seat. *$225.*

A. and B. Matching side and arm chairs with carved crests, seven spindles and caned seats. Left, $250+; Right, $450.

C. Side chair with pressed crest and slat, seven spindles and caned seat. $250.

D. Side chair with pressed crest and slat, six spindles and pressed board seat. $225.

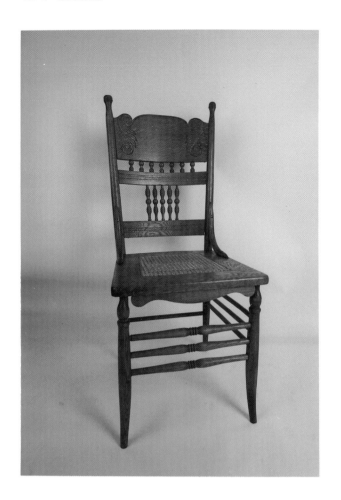

A. Side chair with carved crest, two slats, turned spindles and caned seat. *$225.*

B. Side chair with pressed back, seven spindles and caned seat. Set of 6-*$275 ea.*

C. Side chair with pressed crest, seven spindles and woven seat. *$250.*

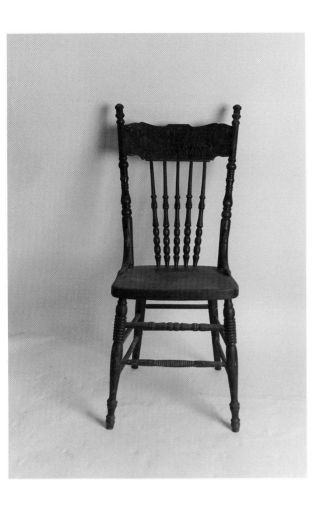

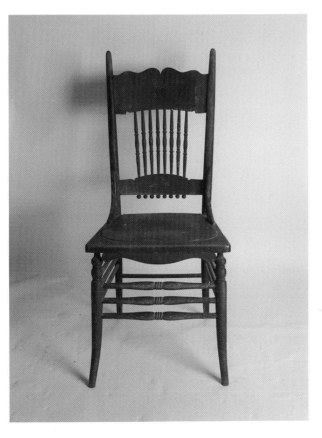

A. Side chair with pressed crest, five spindles and solid seat. Set of 6-*$200 ea.*

B. Side chair with pressed crest, eight spindles and pressed board seat. Set of 6-*$250 ea.*

C. Side chair with carved crest, four spindles, and solid seat. Set of 4-*$125 ea.*

Tables

A. Pedestal extension table with three leaves on octagonal drum pedestal and four splayed legs. *$800.*

B. Round pedestal side table on four scrolled legs. *$275.*

C. round pedestal side table with skirt on four scrolled legs. *$325.*

A. Round pedestal dining table with carved lion's head and paw supports. (with all original leaves), *$4500.*

B. Pedestal extension table with four leaves on tapering drum and four scrolled feet. *$1300.*

C. Side table with four lobed top and skirt on tapering reeded pedestal and four paw feet. Unique shape, very desirable. *$750.*

A. Round table with carved edge on three carved griffin supports and platform bases. *$6500.*

B. Pedestal extension table with seven leaves on a split pedestal and four carved legs with paw feet, made by the Hastings Table Co. of Hastings, Michigan. *$4500.*

A. Round table with carved edge and skirt on four cabriole legs with ball and claw feet, and four matching side chairs with oval paneled backs and solid seats. *$2500 set.*

B. Extension dining table with rectangular top and seven leaves with molded skirt on six turned and reeded legs with ball feet. *$1500.*

C. Extension dining table with rectangular top and carved skirt on five pedestal legs joined by stretchers. *$1800.*

A. Miniature extension dining table with rectangular top and three leaves on five turned and reeded pedestal legs. *$1800.*

B. Extension dining table with rectangular top and seven leaves on six turned legs joined in pairs by stretchers. In this picture, the end pairs of legs are reversed , the stretchers should curve inward. *$1600.*

C. Extension dining table with rectangular top and five leaves, edge and skirt molded, on five turned and reeded legs, the center one with ball foot, the others with paw feet. *$1400.*

D. Oval center table with drawers in the skirt and four supports, two turned and carved and two carved as griffins, all on a shaped platform base with bun feet. *$4000.*

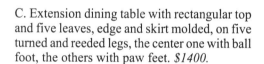

A. Rectangular library table with drawers in the skirt on lyre shaped solid supports and paw feet joined by a shelf. *$850.*

B. Pool table in molded oak frame on octagonal legs and block feet. *$8500.*

C. Rectangular library table with beaded edge, drawer in the skirt, and four turned legs joined by a shelf. *$600.*

A. Rectangular center table with carved skirt on four raking turned legs joined by a shelf and metal claw and glass ball feet. *$800.*

B. Rectangular library table on four spiral turned legs joined by stretchers and a shelf and ending in paw feet. *$750.*

Opposite page:
A. Kidney shaped side table with carved skirt on four shaped legs joined by a shelf with a partial railing as ornamentation. *$375.*

B. Square center table with molded skirt on four splayed turned legs joined by a round shelf and ending in metal claw and glass ball feet. *$250.*

C. Square side table with scrolled ends on four supports joined by a shaped shelf and extending to cabriole legs. *$275.*

D. Heart shaped side table with beaded edge on three splayed turned legs joined by a heart shaped shelf and ending in metal claw and glass ball feet. Very desirable shape. *$550.*

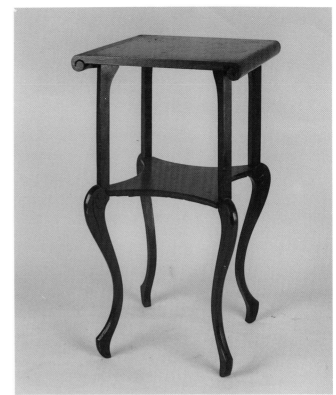

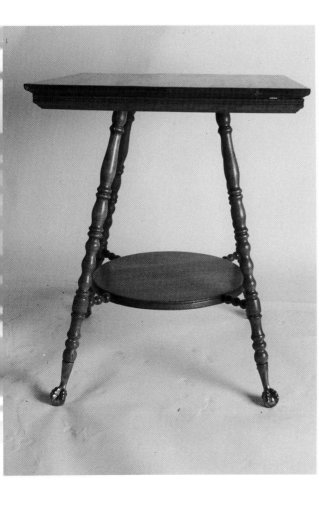

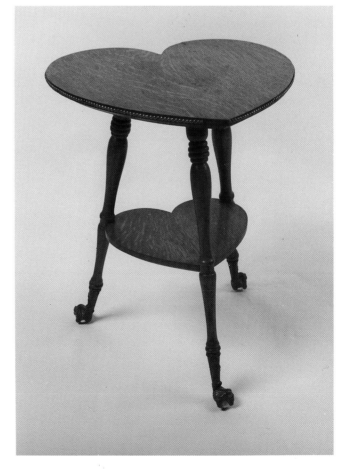

A. Square center table on four twist turned raking legs joined by a shelf and ending in metal claw and glass ball feet. *$300.*

B. Rectangular center table with cut-out skirt on four turned legs joined by a shelf with end ornaments. *$650.*

C. Square center table with turned skirt on four turned raking legs joined by a round shelf and four turned spindles. The legs end in metal claw and ball feet. *$600.*

D. Square center table with pierced skirt on Four turned legs joined by a shelf. *$425.*

A. Oval center table on four flat cabriole legs joined by an oval shelf. *$325.*

B. Low square side table with carved top, scalloped skirt and four carved legs joined by a shelf. *$550.*

C. Library table with rectangular top on four flat cabriole legs joined by stretchers and a shelf. *$475.*

D. Oval center table on four flat cabriole legs joined by a turtle-shaped shelf. *$325.*

Opposite page:
A. Square center table on four raking turned legs joined by a round shelf with gallery and four shaped stretchers. *$275.*

B. Round side table on four turned and raking legs joined by a round shelf. *$375.*

C. Square center table on four turned raking legs joined by four iron brackets and a round shelf with ornamented skirt. *$325.*

D. Square center table with serpentine sides on four turned legs joined by a shaped shelf and ending in metal splayed feet. *$275.*

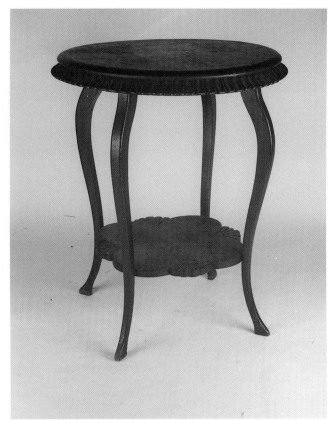

A. Ovoid center table with serpentine edge on four flat cabriole legs joined by a turtle shaped shelf. *$300.*

B. Round center table with carved skirt on four square cabriole legs joined by a lobed and carved shelf. *$350.*

C. Square center table on thin cabriole legs joined by a shaped shelf and ending in paw feet. *$325.*

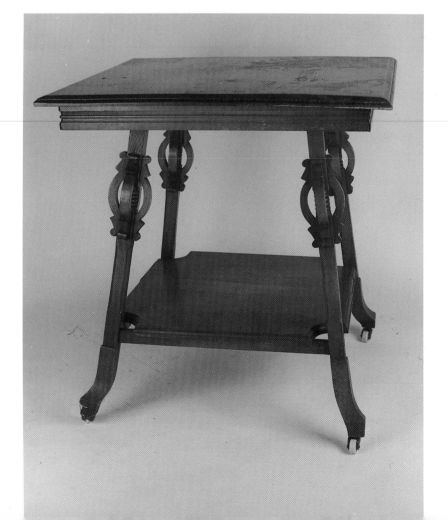

A. Round center table with carved skirt on four round legs joined by a shaped shelf with galleries at two sides. *$600.*

B. Rectangular center table with molded skirt on four square raking legs bearing carved ornaments and joined by a shelf. *$550.*

C. Square center table with serpentine top on cyma-curved supports and turned spindles on two sides joining a shelf which rest on four square tapering legs. *$450.*

Opposite page:
A. Round games table with rotating fitted top and carved edge on four cabriole legs joined by stretchers above the paw feet. *$1400.*

B. Rectangular library table with rounded corners on four cabriole legs. *$500.*

C. Drop leaf side table with carved corners, two drawers and four turned legs. *$750.*

A. Rectangular drawing table on adjustable iron stand and base. *$500.*

B. Rectangular drop leaf table with rounded corners on six straight round legs which end in pad feet. *$950.*

Hall furniture

A. Hat stand with four iron arms on the turned stem and four flat, molded legs. *$450.*

B. Hat stand with six turned hat pegs on the turned stem and four turned legs. (plain) *$150.*

A. Hall stand with carved frame, oval mirror, two double metal hat hooks and compartment in the base. *$2650.*

B. Hall stand with shield shaped mirror, four double metal hat hooks, and compartment in the base. *$2300.*

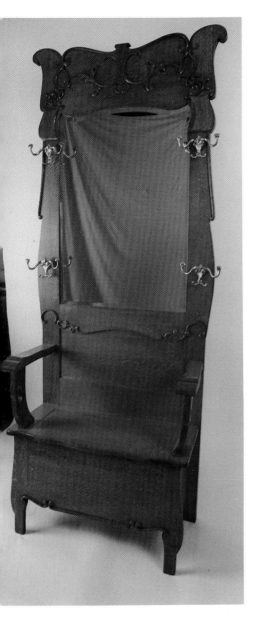

A. Hall stand with carved frame, rectangular mirror arched at the top, four double hat hooks and compartment in the base. *$1500.*

B. Hall stand and pendulum clock with carved frame, two shaped mirrors, four double hat hooks and compartment in the base. Sold at auction, 1997. *$14,500.*

A. Wide hall stand with carved frame, rectangular mirror, four double hat hooks, and compartment in the carved base. *$4200.*

B. Hall stand with carved crest, shaped mirror, four double hat hooks, high side spindles, and compartment in the base. *$3000.*

Opposite page:
A. Hall bench with crest and panels carved with cupid figures, caryatid arm supports, compartment in the base and paw feet. *$4000.*

B. High backed hall bench with Gothic style canopy carving, paneled back, an d solid seat. *$2700.*

C. Hall bench with turned elements, serpentine crest and woven wooden back, solid seat. George Hunzinger Design. *$2800.*

A. Hall stand with three carved back panels, two double hat hooks and compartment in the seat. *$2200.*

B. Plinth with round top, turned and reeded stem, and round base. *$600.*

C. Plinth with round top, turned, reeded and carved stem, and round base. Pineapple carving is desirable. *$750.*

A. Plinth with round top over square block with four carved lion's head masks, turned and carved stem on round base and four paw feet. Outstanding! *$2500.*

B. Plinth with square top and stem carved to include to crouching child figure over the square base. Sits against the wall. Exceptional item! *$8500.*

STICKLEY-BRANDT FURNITURE CO., BINGHAMTON, N. Y.

No. 393

No. 558

Pedestal. Size of top, 14x14 inches. Piano polish. Golden Quartered Oak or Mahogany finish.

Price..............$2.95
$400

Pedestal. Top, 14x14 inches. Golden Quartered Oak or Genuine Mahogany, piano polish.

Oak................$6.50
Mahogany...........7.50
$700

Livingroom Furniture

A. Piano stool with adjustable round seat and four turned legs on metal claw and glass ball feet. *$275.*

B. Bench with upholstered seat, four raking turned legs joined by an H-stretcher. *$225.*

C. Shelf clock with pressed decoration labeled "Butler Brothers, New York" housing a white face clock marked "The Ingraham Co., Bristol, Conn." behind the decorated glass door. *$450.*

D. Two footstools: left, with faces carved into the ends; right, with scalloped top and pierced decorations in the sides. Left, *$675;* Right, *$400.*

E. Bench with laminated dished seat on four turned legs joined by turned stretchers. *$250.*

A. Hanging wall clock with carved decorations and cast metal mounts, white face unsigned. Waterbury Clock is very collectible. *$2800.*

B. Shelf clock with brass face and chiming mechanism, case ornately decorated with cast metal mounts and urn finials. *$1500.*

C. Shelf clock with pressed decoration housing white face pendulum clock, unsigned, with painted portrait on the pendulum, and decorated glass door. *$450.*

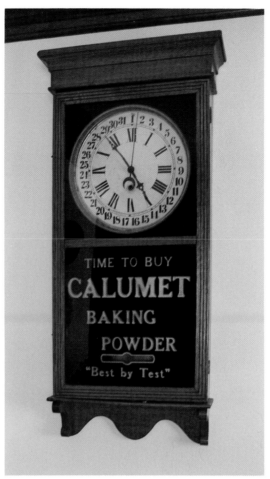

A. Pendulum wall clock in octagonal case, pendulum door lettered "Regulator", white face unmarked. *$550.*

B. Pendulum wall clock in rectangular case with door lettered TIME TO BUY CALUMET BAKING POWDER "Best by Test", white face with date and time mechanism by Sessions. Weight Driven-Good Paint. *$750.*

C. Wall clock with carved frame and enameled tin numerals, mechanism unmarked. Black Forest-*$900.*

D. Pendulum wall clock with round white face marked Seth Thomas, and rectangular weight and pendulum compartment. *$1500.*

A. Detail of hood
B. Detail of waist

C. Detail of base

D. Tall case clock marked Tiffany & Co., New York with brass face, Westminster chimes and elaborate carved detail. Similar sold in 1997, not as nice-no crest. *$22,000.*

A. Tall case clock in open case with brass face set incorrectly here, unmarked. *$1200.*

B. Tall case clock with brass face marked Self Winding Clock Co., New York. The ornamentation is painted gesso applied to the case. *$7500.*

C. Tall case clock with steel face marked Bailey, Banks & Biddle, Philadelphia. *$9000.*

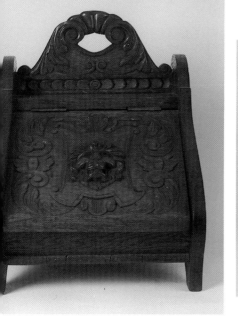

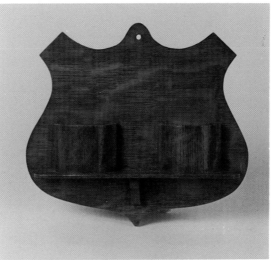

A. Hanging picture frame with carved edges. *$200.*

B. Hanging picture frame with carved and molded border around carved and painted gesso liner. 31 x 34. In perfect condition. *$450.*

C. Coal scuttle with carved decoration on the handle and hinged panel. *$250.*

D. Shield-shaped hanging matches holder with two compartments. *$200.*

E. Two bellows with different carved mark decoration. *$350 ea.*

A. Ceiling-mounted lighting fixture with Greek Key design carved in the frame supporting the leaded glass panels. *$950.*

B. Table lamp of carved base and shade each supporting leaded and stained glass panels. *$1500.*

A. Floor lamp with oak framed shade supporting silk fabric and fringe and turned oak stem on round base. *$500.*

B. Wall sconce with beaded frame around beveled mirror and projecting shelf for a candle. Rare. *$500 ea.-$1200 for a pair.*

C. Pair of candlesticks with brass candle cups, twist turned stems, and round bases. *$150 pair.*

A. Music stand with serpentine door on flat shaped legs. *$375.*

B. Music stand and record cabinet with rectangular solid top and wicker sides and door. *$1200.*

C. and D. Two views of a recordings cabinet, opened to show the stored cylinders, and closed supporting the "Music Master" Edison Recording Machine with speaking horn attached. Superb! *$4500 as a pair-$2000 ea.*

A. The Regina Company's Sublima Piano & Mandolin Orchestra console, mechanical music machine. Rare. *$18,000.*

B. Columbia Granfonia victroloa and music and record cabinet. *$850.*

C. Regina Company's music box with large metal discs. Rare. *$20,000.*

A. Upholstered sofa with frame carved as griffins at the sides. *$8500.*

B. Detail of sofa with griffin carving.

Opposite page:
A. Upholstered and tufted sofa with animal heads on the arms and resting on paw feet. *$1800.*

B. Leather upholstered and tufted day bed with molded frame on carved feet. *$1500.*

Study furniture

A. Fall front desk and bookcase with three drawers on paw feet. *$1500.*

B. Fall front desk with mirror, fitted interior, four drawers and a cabinet in the case resting on tapering legs. *$2000.*

C. Fall front desk with drawer and shelf between the solid end boards. *$650.*

A. Flat top desk with solid gallery on three sides and five drawers in the case, recessed side panels. *$1800.*

B. Flat top desk with extending writing surface fitted interior on four cabriole legs. *$950.*

C. Large flat top desk of oval shape with two side consoles each containing four drawers and two cabinets. *$3600.*

posite page:

Roll top desk with hinged side
...gs, fitted interior and eight draw-
...in the side cases, made by The
...neberger Company, Philadelphia.
...00.

...Large roll top desk with small in-
...or drawers, three long drawers in
... convex skirt and three convex
...wers in each of the side cases
...ch are flanked by pillars. $12,000.

...Small roll top desk with a mirror
... three drawers mounted above
...roll, fitted interior and extending
...e covered writing surface, and
... shelves between the solid side
...rds. Shown on the cover with the
... closed. $1600.

...Large roll top desk with small
...wers and shelves fitted inside, and
...ee drawers in each of the side
...es. $3500.

...Roll top desk with fitted interior
...d three drawers in the case above
...calloped skirt and carved feet.
...00.

...Combination desk and bookcase
...h two mirrors and carved deco-
...on. $2500.

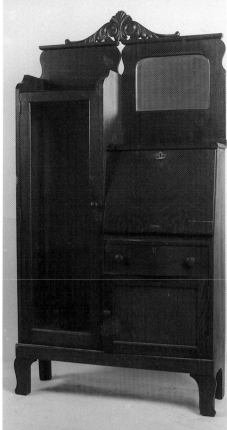

A. through E. These combination desk and bookcase units display the variety of design that is found in this very popular form. Most examples are not marked by the manufacturers, but an exception is 70B (bottom left) which bears the label of Baker and Company of Allegan, Michigan, #116. A. *$2400,* B. *$1800,* C. *$1200,* D.*$1900,* E. Outstanding. *$3500*

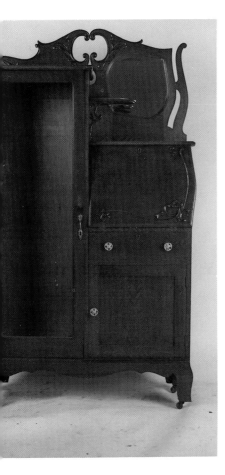

A. through E. Combination desk and bookcase units. A. *$1700*, B.*$2200*, C.*$2400*, D.*$2000*, E. Swing Mirror. *$1900*

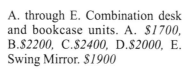

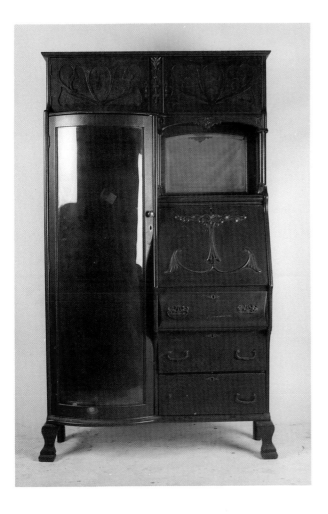

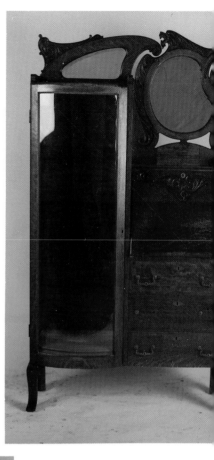

A. through C. Combination desk and bookcase units. A. *$2200,* B. *$4000,* C. *$1900*

D. Round lectern with slanted book rest and paneled sides behind four free-standing columns. *$1800.*

E. Lectern carved as an eagle figure on a pedestal base, with adjustable book rest at the back. (two views). *$8000.*

A. Bookcase in four stacking sections, two with plain glass panel and two with leaded glass panel over a base section with drawer on paw feet. One section labeled "Macey sectional bookcase unit no. 912½ Pat'd. Quartered oak golden. One of a pair shown. *$2500 ea.*

B. Bookcase with flat top molding and leaf carved stiles flanking two glass paneled doors, on paw feet. *$1950.*

C. Tall bookcase with straight cornice molding over two doors with two glass panels in each, on carved skirt and curved feet. *$1900.*

A. Hanging cupboard with open shelf above two glass paneled doors enclosing adjustable shelves and two drawers below. *$1200.*

B. Store case with glass back and sides and six glass paneled doors each enclosed racks for rolls of ribbon. *$1800.*

C. and D. Store case with glass sides and doors enclosing racks for rolls of ribbon, shown opened and closed, labeled "Exhibition Show Case Co., Erie, Ohio, Patented Dec. 31, 1895." *$2200.*

A. Sewing table with case enclosing three drawers and folding leaf supported by two turned legs. *$650.*

B. Thread cabinet of six shallow drawers made to hold Clark thread. Drawer fronts with inset painted panels. *$1000.*

C. Gun case with carved frames of two glass paneled doors enclosing racks for four long barrel guns, ten ammunition drawers and open shelves, with a long drawer in the base. Rare. *$3500.*

D. Thread cabinet of six shallow drawers made to hold thread, the back with an inset pressed panel labeled J. & P. Coates' spool cotton. *$1000.*

Diningroom furniture

A. Miniature sideboard with carved crest, top shelf, ovoid mirror, and three drawers and two doors in the case. *$1600.*

B. Sideboard with three mirrors and two shelves over the case with four drawers and two doors. *$1500.*

C. Sideboard with arched mirror over the case with four drawers and two carved doors on paw feet. *$1700.*

D. Sideboard with carved crest and shelf over rectangular mirror. The case has three drawers and two carved doors. *$1200.*

Opposite page:
A. Sideboard with carved crest and valance over a rectangular mirror and two shelves. The case has three drawers over two paneled doors. *$2200.*

B. Sideboard with carved valance over griffin carvings and mirrors in two tiers with free-standing columns supporting the shelf. The serpentine case has six drawers and four carved doors. *$3600.*

C. Sideboard with carved frame over 3-part mirrored back flanked by carved dolphin figures. The case has two shaped drawers over two paneled doors and a long drawer. *$4000.*

D. Sideboard with carved frame and long shelf over two shelves and a rectangular mirror in the back. The case has three drawers over two carved doors. *$1400.*

A. China cabinet with carved crest, oval top and shelf separated by mirrored back and two carved grifin figures, the oval case with adjustable shelves within rounded glass sides and door, on paw feet. *$7500.*

B. Sideboard with three groups of ornate carving in the crest over four cupboards and three mirrored back panels. The serpentine case has four drawers and five carved doors above the carved skirt. Sold in 1996, *$22,000.*

C. Small sideboard with carved crest and rope molding over rectangular mirrored back and case with glass door over a drawer. *$1100.*

A. Sideboard with carved crest and shelf over rectangular mirror. The case has three drawers and two doors carved with faces. *$2600.*

B. Sideboard with backboard carved with urn, two griffins, and two faces and the case with three drawers over three doors, the center one carved with the head of Bacchus. *$3000.*

C. Sideboard with carved crest including angels over china cupboard with curved glass sides and door, mirrored back panels, and case with four drawers over two carved doors. *$3500.*

D. China cabinet in three sections, the center one with mirrored back and convex glass door, flanked by two flat doors enclosing adjustable shelves, and three drawers in the base. *$6500.*

A. China cabinet with carved canopy and griffin figures over the case with mirrored back and curved glass sides an door. Sold in 1997. *$13,500.*

B. China cabinet with gallery at top and curved glass sides, glass door and four scrolled legs. *$4500.*

C. China cabinet with carved frieze and columns separating the curved glass sides and door, the case on four paw feet. *$4000.*

Opposite page:
A. China cabinet with columns separating the curved glass sides and door, all resting on four paw feet. *$2400.*

B. China cabinet with carved frame and two glass paneled doors over two drawers carved with winged head figures. *$2800.*

C. Wide china cabinet in three sections with carved frieze and end caryatid figures flanking the straight side and convex center glass paneled doors. The case rests on three front feet carved with heads. *$18,000.*

A. China cabinet with carved frame and ovoid mirror above the case with curved glass sides and door on four curved legs. *$2400.*

B. China cabinet with straight glass sides and door panel over cabriole front legs. *$900.*

C. China cabinet with arched mirror over the concave case with curved glass sides and door, on four square shaped legs. *$1400.*

A. China cabinet with mirror over the curved glass sides and door, on four cabriole legs. *$1500.*

B. China cabinet with straight cornice over curved glass sides and serpentine door, all on four cabriole legs. *$1900.*

C. China cabinet with leaf and figure carved arch and caryatid figures between the curved glass sides and straight glass door, all resting on four cabriole legs with paw feet. *$6500.*

A. Two-piece corner cupboard with scroll pediment and flame finials over glass paneled sides and two doors, resting over two carved panel cupboard doors and on claw and ball feet. *$7000.*

B. Two-piece corner cupboard with scroll pediment and flame finials over side columns and arched fifteen paned glass door, resting over two drawers and two cupboard doors, on paw feet. Beautiful! *$8500.*

Opposite page:
A. Corner cupboard with two glass paneled doors over a drawer and two double paneled cupboard doors on a molded base. *$2000.*

B. Two-piece corner cupboard with fluted pilasters flanking the two glass paneled doors over two paneled cupboard doors. *$4500.*

C. One-piece corner cupboard with six glass panes in the upper door over a drawer and double paneled cupboard door. *$4000.*

D. One piece corner china cabinet with ornate carving in the cornice and frame of the flat glass paneled door, standing on four cabriole legs and a back corner support. *$6800.*

A. Flat cupboard with carved cornice over two double paneled doors, an open shelf, two drawers and two double paneled cupboard doors. "John Scott, Leesville, Ohio" painted on the back. *$2500.*

B. Flat cupboard with carved crest over two glass paneled doors, and lower case with two drawers over two paneled cupboard doors. *$3100.*

A. Flat cupboard of ash wood with shaped cornice over two glass paneled doors and an open shelf, the lower case with two drawers over two paneled cupboard doors. *$2500.*

B. Flat cupboard with shaped and carved cornice over two glass paneled doors, the lower case with two drawers over two paneled cupboard doors. *$1900.*

A. Ice box of ornately carved design with oval mirror in the upper door, large lower door and drawer in the base, make by Tacoma Ice Box Company. *$3000.*

B. Ice box with shelves, mirror and two drawers above the case where two doors enclose the "Cork Filled" ice compartment. Parlor Icebox. *$2500.*

C. Insulated ice water cistern of turned top and reeded wood sides around the iron container with spigot. *$650.*

D. Small ice box with three compartments enclosed by doors and a glass panel inscribed "Belding Hall, Notaseme, Stone lined". *$1400.*

A. Wet sink and cupboard with open shelf above two recessed paneled doors and three drawers overhanging the metal lined sink and splash board. The case below has two recessed paneled cupboard doors. *$3000.*

B. Pie safe of oak frame and doors supporting punched tin recessed panels and interior shelves. *$2000.*

C. Hoosier kitchen unit with glass paned doors over a tambour sliding door which encloses a fitted interior. The porcelainized tin work area slides forward and rests over the base where four drawers and a cupboard door are housed. *$1800.*

D. Hoosier kitchen unit labeled "McDougall, Frankfort, Indiana". Three paneled doors and a tambour rolling door enclose a fitted interior over a sliding tin work surface. The base contains five drawers and a cupboard door. *$1700.*

Bedroom furniture

Bedroom suite of ornately carved oak in delicate, ribbon and scroll design. The chests are serpentine with conforming drawers.

A. Double size bed

B. Low chest with mirror

C. High chest with mirror

Set-*$28,000.*

Bedroom suite with strong architectural carved elements and panels. Not shown are matching dressing table and low chest with mirror.

A. Double size bed-*$20,000*.

B. Detail of bed cornice

C. Wardrobe with mirrored door-*$10,000*.

Dressing Table-*$5000*.

Lowchest-*$5000*.

As a set-*$40,000*.

Bedroom suite with shield cartouch in the crests, side pillars and serpentine chests.

A. Chest with large mirror *$4500.*

B. Wash stand with mirror, towel rack and a drawer over cupboard doors. *$3000.*

C. Double size bed *$4500.*

Set-*$12,000.*

Bedroom suite of paneled elements and restrained chip carvings. Set- *$2000.*

A. Wash stand with drawer over two cupboard doors.*$500.*

B. Double size bed *$800.*

C. Chest with attached mirror *$700.*

Bedroom suite with rolled and carved elements.

A. Double size bed *$2000.*

B. Chest with attached mirror and four drawers. *$2000.*

C. Wash stand with towel rack and a drawer over two cupboard doors. *$1000.*

Set-*$5000.*

Bedroom suite of oak with light carved detail and recessed panels.

A. Wash stand with towel rack and case for three drawers and a cupboard door. *$500.*

B. Chest with attached mirror and four drawers. *$900.*

C. Double size bed *$1200.*

Set–*$2600.*

Bedroom suite with plenty of delicately carved leaf and scroll decoration in the crests.

A. Dresser with mirror, serpentine case and five drawers. *$2000.*

B. Double size bed with paneled head and foot sections. *$4500.*

C. Wash stand with towel rack and four drawers over two paneled doors. *$1500.*

Set-*$8000.*

A. Blanket chest with hinged led and sunburst carving on the front, corners bound with metal braces, resting on bun feet. *$650.*

B. and C. Matching dresser and wash stand. The dresser with carved frame and support for the mirror with molded frame around five drawers. The was stand with two drawers over two cupboard doors.

B-*$2000.*

C-*$1000.*

A. Double size bed with rolled top and carved leaves and swag decoration. *$2500.*

B. and C. Matching wash stand and dresser, each with carved frame around mirrors and plain supports over the serpentine case. The was stand over two cabinet doors. The dresser with three small over two long drawers.

B-*$1100.*

C-*$800.*

A. Double size bed with carved scroll and leaf decoration and horizontal paneled head and foot boards. *$900.*

B. Double size bed with carved crest, horizontal paneled head and foot board and reeded stiles. *$900.*

C. Bow front tall chest of five drawers with raised back board. *$600.*

Opposite page:

A. Chest of two small drawers over four long drawers with carved back board. *$700.*

B. Office chest with molded frame around two cabinet doors and six drawers of various sizes. This is a highly unusual form. *$2500.*

C. Chest of drawers with stiles carved as lion heads flanking seven drawers which support carved handles and decorations. *$2000.*

D. Office chest of drawers with molded frame and medallion carving extending over the two cabinet doors and four drawers in the case. *$1800.*

A. Serpentine chest of six drawers with raised back board and rope turned stiles. *$1000.*

B. Chippendale style highboy with scrolled arch pediment over a carved door and ten drawers in the upper case. The lower case has three drawers, a scalloped skirt and cabriole legs. *$4500.*

C. Tall chest of drawers with raised splash board and five drawers. The stiles form the feet. *$550.*

A. Dresser with long oval mirror and three drawers in the bowed chest. *$700.*

B. Dresser with long mirror and two raised drawers over two long drawers in the case. *$1200.*

C. Dresser with rectangular mirror over serpentine chest with four drawers. *$600.*

Opposite page:
A. Dresser with carved frame and rectangular mirror over the chest with three drawers, each with floral chip carving. *$800.*

B. Dresser with wide rectangular mirror over a chest with five drawers. *$950.*

C. Dresser with rectangular mirror over a chest with two convex drawers and two straight long drawers. *$750.*

D. Dresser with shaped frame and rectangular mirror over a chest with four drawers. *$600.*

Opposite page:
A. Dresser with large oval mirror with carved support over chest with five drawers. *$1100.*

B. Dresser with oval mirror in scrolled supports over chest with four drawers. *$1000.*

C. Dresser with rectangular mirror on carved supports over double serpentine chest with four drawers. *$900.*

D. Dresser with carved frame and shaped mirror overdouble serpentine chest with four drawers. *$1000.*

A. Tall chest with oval mirror over bowed case with two small and four long drawers. *$1600.*

B. Tall chest with long oval mirror over serpentine case with six long drawers. *$1800.* If Lingerie-*$2500.*

C. Tall chest with oval mirror over double serpentine case with two small and four long drawers. *$1700.*

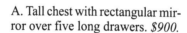

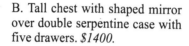

A. Tall chest with rectangular mirror over five long drawers. *$900.*

B. Tall chest with shaped mirror over double serpentine case with five drawers. *$1400.*

C. Tall chest with rectangular mirror over bowed case with five long drawers. *$1000.*

D. Tall chest with rectangular mirror in carved frame and supports over case with five long drawers. *$800.*

E. Tall chest with rectangular mirror in scrolled and carved frame and support over double serpentine case with five drawers. *$1800.*

A. Tall chest with small shaped mirror in scrolled supports over case with two small and four long drawers. *$1200.*

B. Tall chest with arched rectangular mirror over bowed case flanked by pillars and containing four small and four long drawers. *$1900.*

C. Tall chest with rectangular mirror in carved frame over case with two small drawers, a cabinet door and three long drawers. *$1800.*

A. Tall chest with shaped mirror over serpentine case containing four small drawers, a cabinet door and three long drawers, and bearing a stamped label reading "Manufactured by the Widdicomb Furniture Co. Grand Rapids, Michigan" (see detail). *$1800.*

B. Tall chest with rectangular mirror over case with two small drawers, a cabinet door and three long drawers. *$1500.*

C. Tall chest with oval mirror over double serpentine case with two small drawers, cabinet door and three long drawers. *$1900.*

Opposite page:

A. Tall chest with rectangular mirror over case with bowed top drawer, two small drawers, cabinet door and three long drawers. *$1700.*

B. Tall chest with rectangular mirror over a long drawer, two small drawers, cabinet door and two more long drawers. *$1500.*

C. Tall chest with rectangular mirror over case with serpentine top, two small drawers, cabinet door and four long drawers. *$1600.*

D. Combination wardrobe and dresser with recessed paneled closet door, arched mirror and chest with four drawers. *$900.*

A. Matching dressing table and chair, each with heart-shaped mirrors. The table is kidney-shaped with three drawers on cabriole legs, and the chair has a slatted back, round solid seat and pedestal base on four raking legs. Set-*$4500.*

B. Dressing table with oval mirror in carved supports over the double serpentine case with one drawer on cabriole legs. *$1400.*

C. Dressing mirror with carved frame and supports around shaped beveled mirror and projecting serpentine base with one drawer on scrolled feet. *$2900.*

A. Wash stand with long rectangular mirror, two towel racks and case with two drawers and a cabinet door. *$950.*

B. Wash stand with wide rectangular mirror over towel rack and double serpentine case with three drawers and a cabinet door. *$1200.*

C. Wardrobe with carved arched cornice over two mirrored door panels and double serpentine base containing two drawers. *$2500.*

A. Wardrobe with straight cornice molding over two carved and paneled doors and two small drawers on a molded base. *$2000.*

B. Tall wardrobe with scrolled and arched cornice over two carved doors with mirrored panels and central pilaster over two small drawers in the base. *$3000.*

C. Wardrobe with carved arched cornice over one door with shaped mirrored panel and a drawer in the base. The drawer is stamped "Trimmed by No. 6, Varnished April 18, 1909 Mehrten, Inspected May 14, 1909, Stock Roscamp". *$2500.*

Furniture Manufacturers' Catalog Illustrations

The manufacturers' catalogs from which the following illustrations were taken belong to Eileen and Richard Dubrow. They are used with their permission for which the author is grateful.

Chairs

STICKLEY-BRANDT FURNITURE CO., BINGHAMTON, N. Y.

No. 725. Fancy Rocker. Golden Quartered Oak or Mahogany finish. Piano polish.
Each.......................$2.97

$375

No. 723. Fancy Rocker. Golden Quartered Oak or Mahogany finish. Piano polish.
Each.......................$3.25

$375

No. 789. Fancy Rocker. Golden Quartered Oak or Mahogany finish. Piano polish.
Each.......................$3.25

$350

No. 784. Fancy Rocker. Golden Quartered Oak or Mahogany finish. Piano polish.
Each.......................$3.50

$400

No. 4741. Rocker. Golden Quartered Oak or Mahogany finish. Piano polish. A large size Turkish rocker, 35 inches wide and 40 inches high. Upholstered in fine fancy figured velour or tapestry.............................$26.50
Same. In genuine leather.............................$33.50

$500

No. 3390. A large luxurious arm rocker. Upholstered in fine fancy figured velour or tapestry.
Each.............................$23.00
Same. Upholstered in genuine leather.
Each.............................$27.50

$300

No. 4723. Rocker. Golden Quartered Oak or Mahogany finish. Piano polish. Full size Turkish chair with ruffled sides. Upholstered in genuine leather.............................$41.50

$600

THOMPSON, PERLEY & WAITE,

MANUFACTURERS OF

Maple, Oak and Walnut Cane Seat Chairs

CHAMBER SET CHAIRS A SPECIALTY.

BALDWINVILLE, MASS.

WAREROOMS, 84 NORTH STREET, BOSTON

No. 43. *$200*
Geneva Nurse, Brace Arm, veneered.

No. 62. *$150*
Crown Nurse.

No. 68. *$120*
Crown Cottage.

No. 86. *$225*
Crown Rocking.

No. 35. *$150*
Crown Grecian.

No. 4. *$120*
English Cottage.

No. 72. *$200*
Geneva Banister Cottage,
Brace Arm, veneered.

No. 62. B. A. *$225*
Crown Nurse, Brace Arm.

No. 41. *$225*
English Nurse, Brace Arm veneered.

STICKLEY-BRANDT FURNITURE CO., BINGHAMTON, N. Y.

No. 4329. Arm Chair. Golden Quartered Oak or Mahogany finish, piano polish. Tufted seat and back. Upholstered in fancy figured velour, corduroy, imported tapestries or imitation leather.

Each..$11.95
Genuine Leather, each 14.00
$250

No. 3758. Arm Chair or Rocker. Golden Quartered Oak or Mahogany finish, piano polish. Upholstered in fancy figured velour, corduroy, imported tapestries or imitation leather.

Each..$23.00
Genuine Leather, each 26.00
$350

No. 4733. Arm Chair. Golden Quartered Oak or Mahogany finish, piano polish. Upholstered in fancy figured velour, plain corduroy, imported tapestries or imitation leather.

Each..$24.00
Genuine Leather, each 30.00
$400

No. 2358. Full Turkish Rocker. Iron frame. Tufted back and arms. Very large and comfortable. Upholstered in fancy figured velour, plain corduroy, imported tapestries or imitation leather.

Each.. $45.00
Genuine Leather, each................................... 51.50
$350

No. 3341. Full Turkish Rocker. Tufted back and arms. Very large and luxurious. Upholstered in fancy figured velour plain corduroy, imported tapestries or imitation leather.

Each.. $35.00
Genuine Leather, each.................................. 41.00
$400

No. 4025. Turkish Rocker (chair to match). Golden Quartered Oak or Mahogany finish. Upholstered in fancy figured velour, plain corduroy, imported tapestries or imitation leather.

Each.. $33.00
Genuine Leather, each.,................................. 40.00
$450

No. 1767. Turkish Rocker (chair to match). Tufted back and arms. Very large and luxurious. Upholstered in fancy figured velour, plain corduroy, imported tapestries and imitation leather.

Each.. $35.00
Genuine Leather, each.................................. 41.00
$300

No. 4572. Turkish Rocker (chair to match). Golden Quartered Oak or Mahogany finish. Piano polish. Elegantly carved fronts.

Genuine Leather, each.................................$32.50
$900

No. 4075. Full Turkish Chair. Steel frame. Golden Quartered Oak or Mahogany finish. Piano polish. Claw feet. Upholstered in fancy figured velour, plain corduroy, imported tapestries and imitation leather.

Each.. $41.50
Genuine Leather, each 48.50
$600

$300

No. 4562.　Arm Chair $10.75
　　　　　　　Side Chair.. 5.50
$200

$35
No. 4577.　Rocker $16.5
　　　　　　　Side Chair.. 7.5
$25

$300

No. 4562.　Rocker $12.50
　　　　　　　Side Chair.. 5.50
$200

$3.
No. 4577.　Arm Chair $15.0
　　　　　　　Side Chair.. 7.5
$25

No. 4512
In fine grade Velour or Tapestry.

Rocker ....$8.75　　　Side Chair............................$3.75

In Imported Tapestry or Fine Satin Damask.

Rocker ....$10.75　　　Side Chair............................$4.75

$350　　　　　　　　　　　　　　　　　$250

No. 4514
Upholstered in Fine Figured Velour or Tapestry.

Rocker ....$8.75　　　Side Chair............................$3.7

In Upholstered Tapestry or Fine Satin Damask.

Rocker ....$10.75　　　Side Chair............................$4.7

$300　　　　　　　　　　　　　　　　　$25

Tyler Desk Co., St. Louis, Mo.

An Office Chair may wear out, but the Tyler Iron never will.

No. 62. Tyler's New Library.

h Nos. 61 and 63. Antique Oak, Wal-
or Cherry; Cane Seat. Price, F. O. B. **$7 00**
No. 62 A. *$250*
pholstered in Leather............. **10 00**
$350

No. 63. Tyler's New Short Arm.
Antique Oak, Walnut or Cherry; Plain or Em-
bossed Leather Seat and Top. Price,
F. O. B.............................**$12 50**
No. 63 A. *$500*
Same, Perforated Leather over Cane....... **10 50**
No. 63 B. *$600*
Same, Cane Seat......................... **8 50**
$400

No. 61. Tyler's New Antique Chair.
Oak, Walnut and Imitation Mahogany; High
Back Office—Double Frame; Plain or
Embossed Leather Seat and Top. No man
ever sat in an easier chair. Price, F. O. B. **$15 00**
No. 61 A. *$750*
Same, Perforated Leather over cane........ **12 50**
No. 61 B. *$900*
Same, Cane Seat......................... **10 50**
$600

All of our Rotary and Spring Chairs have best Casters fitted complete.

The Tyler Chair Iron, Invented by C. H. Tyler, July 1887,
is the Only Strictly Reliable Iron made.

Guaranteed for twenty years. Will replace free of charge
any Iron or part of Iron that may become defective within twenty
years from date of purchase.
Fitted to any of our own chairs at an extra cost of **$3 00**
Respectfully,
C. H. TYLER, Patentee.
P. S.—Old style Chair Irons as now furnished on office chairs
complete with legs, $3 50, without legs, $2 50 net.

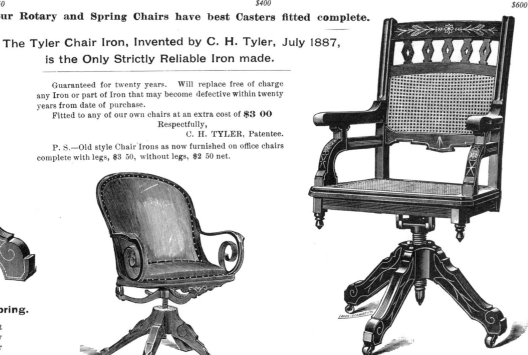

00. Tyler's New Chair Iron and Spring.

tirely of Wrought and Malleable Iron. The most
erful Chair Iron on earth. 2⅜ inch cylinder screw
the spring inside of screw. The entire Chair
complete with legs to fit any ordinary office chair
casters fitted and screws for fastening. Price,
O. B...............................**$5 00**

er, ready for fastening to Chair Seat.
mb Screw for regulating pitch of seat.
rought Iron Bolt.
er and Wheel attached to Spring in Cylinder.
Lug, to prevent Hubbs locking.
ion Ball, to make Spring strong or weak.
eable Iron Hubb, to which legs attach.
nder Screw 2⅜ inch diameter.

No. 392. Tyler's New Congress.

Screw and Spring; Upholstered in Embossed or Plain
Leather; Government Standard; Walnut or Mahogany Finish; Stuffed with Best Curled Hair; Bent
Wood Stock; Highly Finished, and guaranteed to
give entire satisfaction. Price, F. O. B...........**$22 50**
$900

No. 8. Tyler's Full Box Frame Office.
With Tyler's New Screw and Spring attached. Walnut,
Antique Oak or Cherry. Cane Seat and Back. Price, *$650*
F. O. B.............. ....**$12 00**
Full Leather Seat and Back. Price, F. O. B...... **16 00**
The Tyler Iron has no machinery; it is constructed with one
large 2⅜ inch Hollow Screw, Coil Spring and Arm. Absolutely
indestructible; Noiseless; Easy and Graceful motion; Guaranteed
for twenty years.
The Tyler Screw and Spring will be attached to any of our
Chairs for $3 00 extra.

No. 240. Tyler's Revolving and Tilting.

Walnut or Mahoganized Cherry. Weight,
  40 lbs. Price, F. O. B.............. **$9 00**
                                                    $600
                    240 A.
Same, Full Leather...................... **13 50**
                                                    $900
If Tyler Iron and Base, add **$3 00**

No. 229. Dining Chair.

Walnut or Mahoganized Cherry. Price, in *$150*
  Cane, F. O. B...................... **$2 50**
Leather Seat and Back............ ...... **5 50**
                                                    $200

No. 229½ Library Chair.

Walnut or Mahoganized Cherry. Price, in *$250*
  Cane, F. O. B...................... **$5 5**
Full Leather Seat and Back **9 0**
                                                    $300

All of our Rotary Chairs have best Casters fitted complete.

F. E. STUART.

Sett Chairs.   Oak or Maple.

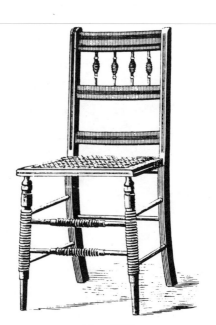

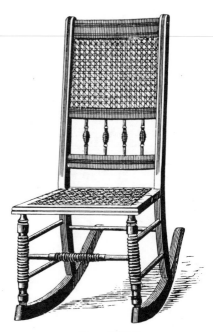

No. 158
$150

No. 158½
$200

No. 136
$150

F. E. STUART.

FOLDING CHAIR.
Slat Seat.

FOLDING CHAIR.
Folded.

BENT PILLAR CHAIR.
With Book Rack for Vestry use.

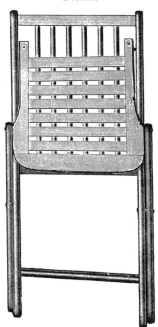

No. 146
$75

No. 146

No. 13½ R
$175

F. E. STUART.

OPERA SETTEES.

These cuts should be transposed.

A. C. RUSSELL

$200
No. 149

Movable Chair, Maple or Birch, finished light or stained.
rpentine seat, fastened with iron pins, and lifts independently.
as rubber stops, covered with perforated veneer or other
aterial, and pack away closely when not in use. A light.
rable and comfortable seat.

$300
No. 149½

Same as 149, only Queen Anne Top.

Oak or Maple.

Tables

We know of no Tables Equal to those made by Tyler Desk Co. of St. Louis, Mo.

Nos. 1 & 3. Tyler's Fine Office Tables. Walnut, Antique Oak or Cherry.

5-Ply Built-up Tops, Covered with Billiard Cloth, Best Locks, Portable, Shipped K. D., Boxed, Casters Fitted.

No. 1. Size, 52 in. by 32 in.
Price, F. O. B. (Weight, 60 lbs.)..........$13 00
$900
No. 3. Size, 42 in. by 28 in.
Price, F. O. B. (Weight, 50 lbs.)........... 12 00
Brass Corners Fitted, if desired, at $2.50 extra per set net.
$800

No. 6. Tyler's Fancy Table. Walnut, Antique Oak or Cherry.

24 inches wide and 36 inches long, One Drawer, Covered with Cloth or Polished Wood Top.

Price, F. O. B. $8 50
$800

Nos. 4 & 5. Tyler's Extra Fine Library Tabl... Walnut, Antique Oak or Cherry.

5-Ply Built-up Tops and Square Legs, Cov... with Billiard Cloth, A 1 Locks, Casters Fitted, Ship... K. D., Boxed, Weight, 70 lbs.

No. 5. Size, 3 ft. 6 in. by 2 ft. 4 in.
Price, F. O. B.............................$14...
No. 4. Size, 4 ft. 4 in. by 2 ft 8 in.
Price, F. O. B......................... ... 16...
Brass Corners Fitted, if desired, at $2.50 extra per net.

No. 2 & 7. Fine Office Tables. Walnut, Antique Oak, Cherry.

5-Ply Built-up Tops, Covered with Billiard Cloth, Best Locks, Portable, Shipped K. D., Boxed, Casters Fitted.
$1000
No. 2. Size, 5 ft. by 32 in. Weight, 90 lbs. Price, F. O. B.........$14 50
No. 7. Size, 6 ft. by 34 in. Weight, 100 lbs. Price, F. O. B.......... 17 00
Brass Corners Fitted, if desired, at $2.50 extra per set net. $1100

Tyler's Square Leg R. R. or Office Table. Solid Walnut or Che...

Covered with Heavy Rubber Duck, Paneled Top, Veneered Fronts. Three Sizes carried in Stock.
No. 24. 4 ft. long by 32 in. wide. Price, F. O. B . $1000 ....$ 9...
No. 25. 5 ft. long by 32 in. wide. Price, F. O. B........$1200......... 10...
No. 26. 6 ft. long by 32 in. wide. Price, F. O. B.............. $1400. 12...
Extra Lengths to Order at $1.50 per foot.

Nos. 16 & 17 – Tyler's Extra Fine Office or Directory Tables.

5-Ply Built-up Top and Solid Brass Corners. Walnut, Antique Oak or Cherry. Covered with Billiard Cloth; A 1 Locks; 5 Large Legs; Casters fitted; Shipped K. D., Boxed.
$1600
No. 16. Size, 7 ft. long by 34 in. wide; weight, 130 lbs., Price, F. O. B. $28 00
No. 17. Size, 8 ft. long by 34 in wide; weight, 150 lbs., Price, F. O. B. 30 00
$1800

Nos. 18, 19 & 20. Tyler's Extra Fine Office or Directory Tables.

5 Ply Built-up Top; 5 Large Carved Legs; Crescent Base; Solid Brass Corners. Walnut, Antique Oak or Cherry. Covered with Billiard Cloth; A 1 Locks; Casters fitted; Shipped K. D., Boxed.

No. 18. Size, 6 ft. long by 34 in. wide, weight. 110 lbs., Price, F. O. B. $27...
No. 19. Size, 7 ft. long by 34 in. wide, weight, 130 lbs., Price, F. O. B. 30...
No. 20. Size, 8 ft. long by 34 in. wide, weight, 150 lbs., Price, F. O. B. 34...

$2000 $2200 $2400

All of our Tables have Best Casters Fitted.

STICKLEY-BRANDT FURNITURE CO., BINGHAMTON, N. Y.

A PAGE FULL OF PARLOR TABLE BARGAINS

(While the cuts are small, the Tables are all regular table height.)

No. 289. Top 14x14.
Each.................97c
No. 289 1-2. Same with
brass claw feet...**$1.45**

No. 288. Top 20x20.
Each..............**$1.45**
No. 288 1-2. Same with
brass claw feet...**$1.95**

No. 287. Top 24x24.
Each...............**$1.85**
No. 287 1-2. Same with brass
claw feet.............**$2.35**

No. 286. Top 28x28.
Each.............**$3.50**
No. 286 1-2. Same with brass
claw feet.............**$5.00**

No. 285. Top 24x36, with a drawer
14x20 inches.
Each..............................**$5.75**
No. 285 1-2. Same with brass claw
feet..................................**$7.25**

No. 284. Top 14x14.
Each. **$1.10**

No. 283. Top 20x20.
Each...............**$1.45**

All these Tables are made in Solid Golden Oak.   Well made and well finished.   The claw feet are of brass with a solid glass ball.

No. 282. Top 24x24.
Each....................**$1.60**

No. 281. Top 28x28.
Each......... ....**$3.75**

No. 280. Top 24x36, with a drawer
14x20 inches.
Each...................... **$5.75**

No. 229. Top 14x14.
Each................**$1.85**

No. 228. Top 20x20.
Each...............**$2.65**

No. 227. Top 24x24.
Each...............**$3.35**

These Tables are all Solid Golden Oak, well made and well finished.

The three Tables, Nos. 229, 228 and 227, are of Golden Quartered Oak with a piano polish. Handsomely carved rim and French legs.

No. 226. Top 28x28.
Each... ....**$5.75**

No. 225. Top 24x36, drawer 14x20.
Each.................... ....**$9.25**

No. 239 1-2. Top 14x14.
Each................**$2.35**
No. 239. Without
claw feet.....**$1.85**

No. 238. Top 20x20.
Each.............**$2.65**
No. 238 1-2. Same with
claw feet.........**$3.65**

No. 237. Top 24x24
Each............**$3.35**
No. 237 1-2. Same with claw
feet.... ....**$4.35**

No. 236. Top 28x28.
Each............**$5.75**
No. 236 1-2. Same with claw
feet........ ....**$7.25**

These Tables are all Golden Quartered Oak with Piano Polish.

No. 235. Top 24x36, drawer 14x
20. Each.....................**$9.25**
No. 235 1-2. Same with claw
feet.... ....**$10.75**

No. 219. Top 16x16.
Each.... ....**$1.85**

No. 218. Top 20x20.
Each... ....**$2.65**

No. 217. Top 24x24.
Each **$3.35**

No. 216. Top 28x28.
Each **$5.75**

No. 215. Top 24x36, drawer
14x20.
Each....................**$9.25**

These Tables are all Golden Quartered Oak and Piano Polish.

No. 209. Top 16x16.
Each...........**$1.50**
No. 209 1-2. Same
with claw feet.**$2.00**

No. 208. Too 20x20.
Each..........**$2.35**
No. 208 1-2. Same
with claw feet.**$2.85**

No. 207. Top 24x24.
Each...........**$2.95**
No. 207 1-2. Same
with claw feet.**$3.95**

No. 206. Top 28x28.
Each..........**$5.00**
No. 206 1-2. Same with
claw feet.........**$6.50**

No. 205. Top 24x36.
Each **$9.25**
No. 205 1-2. Same with claw
feet.... ....**$10.75**

No. 169. Top 16x16.
Each.......... **$2.10**

No. 168. Top 20x20.
Each........ ..**$2.90**

No. 167. Top 24x24.
Each...............**$3.60**

These Tables are all made in Golden Quartered Oak with Piano Polish.

No. 166. Top 28x28.
Each...... ....**$6.50**

No. 165. Top 24x36.
Each...................**$10.25**

No. 179. Top 16x16.
Each.............**$2.10**
No. 179 1-2. Same
with claw feet.**$2.60**

No. 178. Top 20x20.
Each.............**$2.90**
No. 178 1-2. Same
with claw feet.**$3.40**

No. 177. Top 24x24.
Each.............**$3.60**
No. 177 1-2. Same with
claw feet.........**$4.60**

No. 176. Top 28x28.
Each............**$6.50**
No. 176 1-2. Same
with claw feet.........**$8.00**

No. 175. Top 24x36.
Each.................**$10.25**
No. 175 1-2. Same with claw
feet.....................**$11.75**

These Tables are made from the best selected Golden Quartered Oak and have a Piano Polish.

First row left to right: top then bottom; $150, $200, $250, $300, $275, $350, $350, $400, $375, $400, $150, $175
Second row: $125, $150, $225, $150, $175, $200
Third row: $300, $375, $150, $200, $200, $250, $250, $300, $300, $375
Fourth row: $400, $450, $200, $250, $300, $350, $350
Fifth row: $200, $250, $250, $300, $300, $375, $350, $400, $400, $475, $200, $250, $300
Sixth row: $225, $300, $250, $300, $300, $375, $375, $400, $400, $450, $500, $550

No. 39. ORNAMENTAL TABLE.
$1000

Length, 3 feet; width, 24 inches.

A pleasing Design, in Ionic style. Carved Base and fluted Columns. Wood top.

Walnut, Imitation Mahogany, Quartered Oak, or Mahogany.

No. 143. ORNAMENTAL TABLE.
$1100

Length, 30 inches; width, 30 inches.

A finely carved Modern Antique, with massive proportions. Wood top.

Walnut, Quartered Oak, or Mahogany.

No. 166. ORNAMENTAL TABLE.
$1800

Length, 35 inches; width, 24 inches.

Molded Rim, and Shelf. Turned and molded Legs, with carved Feet. Wood to

Walnut, Imitation Mahogany, Quartered Oak, or Mahoga

No. 139. ORNAMENTAL TABLE.
$900

Length, 27 inches; width, 27 inches.

Renaissance in full detail, with rich Carving.

Walnut, Imitation Mahogany, Quartered Oak, or Mahogany.

No. 150. ORNAMENTAL TABLE.
$1000

Length, 40 inches; width, 29 inches.

Romanesque style, with massive and beautiful proportions. Wood top.

Walnut, Quartered Oak, or Mahogany.

No. 142. ORNAMENTAL TABLE.
$850

Length, 26 inches; width, 26 inches.

Molded Rim. Heavy, spiral Columns. Brass, claw Feet, holding wooden Balls. W

Walnut, Imitation Mahogany, Quartered Oak, or Mahog

No. 30. ORNAMENTAL TABLE.
$650

Length, 28 inches; width, 28 inches.

Modern antique style. Spiral turning on Legs, with carved feet. Wood top.

Walnut, Imitation Mahogany, Quartered Oak, or Mahogany.

No. 26. ORNAMENTAL TABLE.
$700

Length, 24 inches; width, 24 inches.

Top engraved; molded Shelf. Spiral turning on Legs. Wood top.

Walnut, Imitation Mahogany, Quartered Oak, or Mahogany.

No. 100. ORNAMENTAL TABLE.
$750

Length, 26 inches; width, 26 inches.

Attractive design, in Romanesque Style. Carved Columns, and Feet. Wood

This Table is also made with heavy brass claw Feet, holding glass balls, and is num

Walnut, Imitation Mahogany, Quartered Oak, or Mahog

No. 152. ORNAMENTAL TABLE.
$700

Length, 26 inches; width, 26 inches.

Engraved Rim and Shelf. Spiral turning on Legs. Wood top.

nut, Imitation Mahogany, Quartered Oak, or Mahogany.

No. 18. ORNAMENTAL TABLE.
$950

Length, 30 inches; width, 30 inches.

Egyptian composite in new outline and rich Carving. Wood top.

Walnut, Imitation Mahogany, Quartered Oak, or Mahogany.

No. 153. ORNAMENTAL TABLE.
$700

Diameter of Top, when open, 3 feet; when closed, 13 inches.

Modern antique style, with new construction. Wood top.

Walnut, Imitation Mahogany, Quartered Oak, or Mahogany.

No. 26½. ORNAMENTAL TABLE.
$800

Length, 30 inches; width, 30 inches.

Top engraved; molded Shelf. Spiral turning on Legs. Wood top.

Walnut, Imitation Mahogany, Quartered Oak, or Mahogany.

No. 161.   CENTER TABLE.
$800

Length, 30 inches: width, 20 inches.

Grecian style, with modern cluster Base. Marble, or Wood Top.

Walnut, Imitation Mahogany, or Quartered Oak.

No. 27. ORNAMENTAL TABLE.
$600

Length, 24 inches; width, 24 inches.

Engraved Rim and molded Shelf. Spiral turning on Legs. Wood top.

Walnut, Imitation Mahogany, Quartered Oak, or Mahogany.

No. 47. ORNAMENTAL TABLE.
$650

Length, 30 inches; width, 30 inches.

Molded Rim and Shelf. Fluted columns. Wood top.

ut, Imitation Mahogany, Quartered Oak, or Mahogany.

No. 79. ORNAMENTAL TABLE.
$450

Length, 26 inches; width, 20 inches.

Molded Rim, and Shelf. Turned Legs. Wood top.

Walnut, Imitation Mahogany, Quartered Oak, or Mahogany.

No. 14. ORNAMENTAL TABLE.
$900

Length, 32 inches; width, 22 inches.

Richly carved Base, with Shelf. Wood top.

Walnut, Imitation Mahogany, Quartered Oak, or Mahogany.

Sofas

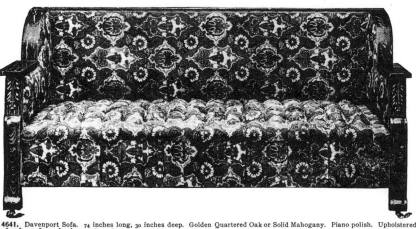

No. 4641. Davenport Sofa. 74 inches long, 30 inches deep. Golden Quartered Oak or Solid Mahogany. Piano polish. Upholstered in fine fancy figured velour or tapestry.
Oak...................................$38.50   Mahogany..................................$40.00
Same. Upholstered in imported tapestry, Roman silk velour, Bokhara velour or Verona velour.
Oak...................................$50.00   Mahogany..................................$55.00

$800

No. 4577. Five Pieces. Mahogany finish, piano polish. Tufted backs, fu~~ edges. Elegantly carved. In fancy figured velours, plain corduroys, fine sa~~ ask, imported tapestries and silk plush, 5 pieces ....
Sofa is 53 inches long..
Se~~

No. 4683. Davenport Sofa. 81 inches long, 31 inches deep. Golden Quartered Oak or Mahogany finish. Piano polish. Upholstered in fine fancy figured velour or tapestry...$50.00
Same. Upholstered in imported tapestry, Roman silk velour, Bokhara velour or Verona velour................................$55.00

$1900

No. 4288. Davenport Sofa. 79 inches long, 32 inches deep. Genuine Mahogany with Crotch Mahogany top. Upholstered in fine fancy figured velour or tapestry...$54.00
Same. Upholstered in imported tapestry, Roman silk velour, Bokhara velour or Verona velour................................$77.00

$2400

No. 4512. Five Pieces. Golden Quartered Oak or Mahogany finish. Piano polish. Sp~~ Upholstered in fine grade of figured velour or tapestry...................................
Sofa..
Five Pieces in Imported Tapestry or Satin Damask..... ....
Sofa..

Set~~

CKLEY-BRANDT FURNITURE CO., BINGHAMTON, N. Y.

768. Victoria Couch. Both ends let down at any angle and independent of each
er. Turkish tufted, claw feet, spring edges, 24 inches deep, 6r inches long when
ed.

....	$16.50	F...............	$18.75	M............	$26.50
....	17.25	H...............	20.75	Pantasote........	28.00
....	18.00	K...............	23.25	Genuine leather..	37.00

$1500

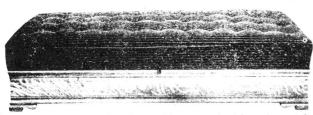

o. 826 1-2. Box Couch. Top lifts up, golden quartered oak frame, button tufted,
ring edges, 31 inches wide, 74 inches long, with self-opening spring. (See descrip-
on below.)

D...........	$15.50	A...............	$19.50	D...............	$21.00
D............	16.00	B...............	20.00	F...............	21.75

Same with frame all covered and no wood showing, 30 inches wide, 74 inches long:

D............	$12.50	A...............	$14.50	D...............	$19.50
D............	13.25	B...............	17.00	F........	22.50

Deduct 75c. net if you do not want the self-opening spring. *$800*

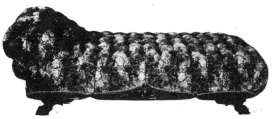

582. Turkish Couch. Deep tufted, golden quartered oak frame, claw feet, hand-
ly carved, full spring edges, 30 inches wide, 82 inches long.

....	$15.50	F...............	$19.25	M	$26.00
....	16.25	H...............	21.25	Pantasote.....	27.50
....	17.25	K...............	23.50	Genuine leather..	39.50

$1100

679. Turkish Couch. Deep tufted, golden quartered oak, elegantly carved, full
g edges, 31 inches wide, 82 inches long.

....	$15.95	F...............	$19.25	M	$26.75
....	16.75	H...............	21.50	Pantasote........	28.50
....	17.50	K...............	24.00	Genuine leather..	41.00

$1200

No. 602. LION HEAD ARMS.

Walnut or Oak Frame. This gives a perfect Spring Bed. Size. 4 feet by 6½ feet.

$1200

WHAT IS THE HOME COMFORT SOFA BED?

IT IS THE

✤OTT PATENT PARLOR SOFA BED.✤

No. 13. DOUBLE FACED COUCH.

Walnut or Oak Frame. Hard Edge. Size 5 feet 10 inches by 24 inches.
Fitted with Fox Patent Casters.

$900

No. 16½. DOUBLE FACED COUCH.

Walnut or Oak Frame. Spring Edge. Size 6 feet by 24 inches, and 6 feet by 26 inches.
Fitted with Fox Patent Casters.

$1500

No. 55. SINGLE LOUNGE.

Walnut or Oak Frame. Spring Edge. Banded Front and Back. Full Size Lounge.
Fitted with Fox Patent Casters.

$2500

Desks

No. 91. DESK.

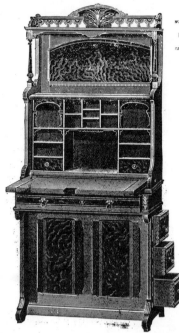

Length, 32 inches; width, 18 inches; height, 4½ feet.

A beautiful Design in Colonial style.   Richly carved Front.
Paneled Ends.   Five Drawers, locks, and keys.

Walnut, Imitation Mahogany, or Quartered Oak

$1800

No. 212 FALL LEAF PARLOR DESK.

Size, 30x18 inches.

Walnut, Cherry or Oak, writing part covered with Billiard Cloth.

If desired, will put plain mirror in top in place of veneered panel, at same price

Price—In white, $17.00; finished, $22.00.

The same desk with bevel French mirror in top, $24.00.   *$2400*

No. 211 FALL LEAF PARLOR DESK.

Size, 30x18 inches.

Walnut, Cherry or Oak, writing part covered with Billiard Cloth.

Price—In white, $13.00; finished, $18.00.   *$1800*

Tyler Desk Co., St. Louis, Mo.

**No. 225. Tyler's Library Desk. Walnut, Antique
Oak or Cherry.**

Size, 34 in. wide, 24 in. deep, 37 in. high to top of back; cloth trimmed; oil finish; portable. Weight, 75 lbs.

Price, F. O. B **$13 00**
$1200

**No. 228. Tyler's Library Desk. Walnut, Antique
Oak or Cherry.**

Size, 36 in. wide, 26 in. deep, 48 in. high to top of back; shelves 10x7; clo
15x11x8½ inside, pigeon holes and book spaces.   Cloth trimmed; finish; portable. Weight, 90 lbs.

Price, F. O. B **$20 00**
$1200

Tyler Desk Co., St, Louis, Mo.

817. Tyler's Bevel Top Table Desk. Walnut or Cherry.

inches wide, 43 inches long. Finished
ck; made with Knock-Down Castings;
e Finish; Covered with Rubber Drill.
ight, 60 lbs. Price, F. O. B..........**$10 00**
$800

No. 106. Tyler's Walnut or Cherry Table Desk.

Size, 43 x 30 inches. Finished Back; Bevel Top;
Covered with Green Felt Cloth or Rubber
Duck; Wood Drawer Pulls. Weight, 60 lbs.
Price, F. O. B.........................**$9 00**
$900

No. 219. Walnut, Oak or Cherry.

Size, 28 inches long, 21 inches deep. Handsome
and Well Finished Desk. Price, F. O. B.. **$6 50**
$800

359. Tyler's Bevel Top Table Desk. Walnut or Cherry.

eet 6 inches by 2 feet 7 inches. Two Drawers; Plain Back; Top
red with Rubber Duck. Weight, 75 lbs. Price, F.O.B........**$11 00**
$1200

No. 220. Tyler's Library Desk. Walnut, Cherry or Antique Oak.

Size, 28 inches wide, 21 inches deep, 34 inches high to Top of Back.
Cloth Trimmed; Oil Finish. Portable. Weight, 60 lbs. Price,
F. O. B..**$10 00**
$1000

NORTHWESTERN FURNITURE CO., Burlington, Iowa.

No. **319**—Class B. 54 in. long, 46 in. deep. *Double* Desk. Made in Walnut, Oak or Cherry.
$1200   Oak in either Antique or 16th Century finish. 3-ply framed, figured Oak top
on Walnut or Cherry. Solid quartered Oak top on Oak. Has eight drawers
on one side and five drawers and one closet on opposite side. Seven
partitioned drawers. Automatic lock with one key locks a tier of drawers.

The Best Tables on the Market for Offices, Hotels, Reading Rooms, Libraries, Directors' Meetings

No. 927

Plain Oak.		Quartered Oak.	
48 inches long 28 inches wide 3 inch leg	$ 6.50 $800	48 inches long 28 inches wide 3 inch leg	$ 8.25 $1000
60 inches long 30 inches wide 4 inch leg	8.50 $1000	60 inches long 30 inches wide 4 inch leg	11.50 $1200
72 inches long 34 inches wide 4 inch leg	10.50 $1200	72 inches long 34 inches wide 4 inch leg	13.75 $1400
84 inches long 40 inches wide 5 inch leg	13.00 $1400	84 inches long 40 inches wide 5 inch leg	17.50 $1600
96 inches long 44 inches wide 5 inch leg	14.50 $1600	96 inches long 44 inches wide 5 inch leg	19.75 $2000

No. 942

Drawers have Hand Carved Pulls as shown in Cut.

Plain Oak.		Quartered Oak.	
52 inches long 30 inches wide 3 inch leg 2 drawers	$10.00 $1000	52 inches long 30 inches wide 3 inch leg 2 drawers	$13.00 $1200
60 inches long 30 inches wide 4 inch leg 2 drawers	12.00 $1200	60 inches long 30 inches wide 4 inch leg 2 drawers	15.50 $1400
72 inches long 34 inches wide 4 inch leg 2 drawers	14.00 $1400	72 inches long 34 inches wide 4 inch leg 2 drawers	18.50 $1600
84 inches long 40 inches wide 5 inch leg 3 drawers	18.75 $1600	84 inches long 40 inches wide 5 inch leg 3 drawers	23.50 $1800
96 inches long 44 inches wide 5 inch leg 3 drawers	20.50 $2000	96 inches long 44 inches wide 5 inch leg 3 drawers	26.00 $2400

Flat Top Office and Library Desks

$1200

No. 910. Solid Golden Oak, 46 inches long, 29 inches deep, well made and well finished................................ $13.00

No. 918 1-2. Same as 910, but with one tier of drawers (see No. 7-42), 42 inches long, Solid Golden Oak, drawer under knee space $11.00

$1000

No. 7-50

DESCRIPTION. Solid Golden Oak, piano polish, beveled and cross paneled, double base, drawer in knee space with separate lock. Combination locks like No. 7-42. Book drawer in lower right hand tier. (See No. 7-42.)

$1500 50 inches long, 32 inches deep $16.25
$1800 55 inches long, 32 inches deep................. 18.75
$1200 60 inches long, 32 inches deep................. 19.50

No. 7-42. Solid Golden Oak, piano polish, beveled and cross panels, double base. Drawer in knee space (which has a separate lock), Combination lock. Top drawer being locked with key, locks all the rest. Two bottom drawers make one large book drawer. 42 inches long, 32 inches deep.................... $14.00

$1250

$3800

No. 12. This is a double desk, having the same arrangement of drawers on each side. A great lawyer's desk. Piano polish, beveled cross panels, combination locks, large drawer in center. Golden Quartered Oak or Solid Mahogany.

60 inches long, 48 inches deep, Oak $46.75 Mahogany $ 67.00
66 inches long, 54 inches deep, Oak 60.00 Mahogany 96.00
72 inches long, 60 inches deep, Oak 78.00 Mahogany 120.00

No. 14. Same as No. 12. In Golden plain Oak only.

55 inches long, 48 inches deep............................. $32.00
60 inches long, 48 inches deep............................. 36.50

$4500

No. 6-50

DESCRIPTION. Golden Quartered Oak or Solid Mahogany, both woods carefully selected. Hand-carved drawer pulls, double base. Combination locks, book drawer in right hand tier. Beveled and cross paneled, 5-ply writing bed.

OAK.

42 inches long, 32 inches wide...... ... . $17.25
50 inches long, 32 inches wide.................. 20.25
55 inches long, 32 inches wide.................. 23.00
60 inches long, 32 inches wide 26.00

42 in. $1000, 50 in. $1200, 55 in. $1400, 60 in. $2000.

MAHOGANY.

42 inches long, 32 inches wide...... ... . $28.00
50 inches long, 32 inches wide......... .... 31.50
55 inches long, 32 inches wide.................. 36.00
60 inches long, 32 inches wide.................. 39.00

STICKLEY-BRANDT FURNITURE CO., BINGHAMTON, N. Y.

We Are Headquarters in Office Furniture

We issue a Special Desk Catalog which we would be pleased to send you.

No. 914. Roll Top Desk. Interior has the regular pigeon hole construction, Solid Golden Oak. 30 inches long. Large drawer under writing bed.
Price........................ ....$8 75

Also a good typewriter desk. **$950**

No. 25. High roll top. Beveled cross panels, large deep drawer in the middle, with separate lock. Combination locks. Adjustable partitions on the inside of the drawers. Double base. All sizes are 32 in. deep and 50 in. high.
Length, 42 in. Price, Oak...$21 00
Length, 50 in. Price, Oak.. 22 00
Length, 55 in. Price, Oak.. 27 00
Length, 60 in. Price, Oak.. 30 50

No. 1. Same as No. 25, but with beautiful figured Golden Quartered Oak. The drawer-pulls are hand-carved, the same as on No. 8. The drawers are finished on the inside, while the depth is 34 inches. The Mahogany is of the best quality.
Length, 42 in. Oak..........$26 75 Mahogany..........$44 00
Length, 50 in. Oak.......... 29 50 Mahogany.......... 50 00
Length, 55 in. Oak.......... 35 50 Mahogany.......... 56 00
Length, 60 in. Oak.......... 39 00 Mahogany.......... 62 00
Length, 66 in. Oak.......... 44 50 Mahogany.......... 74 00

No. 13. High top roll. Double base. Beveled cross panels. Large, deep drawer in center. Combination locks. Enclosed pigeon-hole cases. Each size is 34 in. deep and 50 in. high. Fine polished Golden Oak.
Length, 50 in. Price..$32 00
Length, 55 in. Price.. 35 25
Length, 60 in. Price.. 39 75

No. 912. Roll top. Solid Golden Oak. 42 in. long, 45 in. high. Combination locks. Extension slide. Interior is like No. 911.
Price........... ....$12 75
$1600

No. 125. High roll top. Beveled cross panels. Double base. Combination locks. Large drawer in center with separate lock. Enclosed pigeon-holes. Letter file on inside left hand drawer. All sizes are 32 in. deep and 50 in. high. Golden Oak, piano polish.
Length, 50 in. Price....................................$28 00
Length, 55 in. Price........ .... 32 25
Length, 60 in. Price....................................... 35 50

No. 11. High top roll. Beveled cross panels. Golden Quartered Oak or Solid Mahogany. Piano polish. Hand-carved drawer pulls. Large, deep drawer in center. Letter file on left hand inside drawer. Enclosed pigeon-hole cases. All sizes are 35 in. deep and 50 in. high.
Length, 50 in. Oak......$35 00 Mahogany..............$55 00
Length, 55 in. Oak....... 37 00 Mahogany.............. 60 00
Length, 60 in. Oak....... 45 00 Mahogany.............. 66 00

No. 911. Roll top. Solid Golden Oak. 46 in. long, 46 in. high. Combination locks. Extension slides.
Price........ ....$17 00
$2200

No. 20. High roll top. Beveled cross panels. Double base. Enclosed pigeon-hole cases and rounded filing drawers. Vertical letter file in left end. Eight handy small drawers. Large deep drawer in center. Golden Oak, polish finish. All sizes are 35 in. deep and 50 in. high.
Length, 50 in. Price $36 50
Length, 55 in. Price 39 75
Length, 60 in. Price 44 50

No. 4. Same as No. 20, but in elegant Golden Quartered Oak and Solid Mahogany and with hand-carved drawer-pulls. Also four long letter file drawers down left side.
Length, 50 in. Oak. ....$39 00 Mahogany..........$63 00
Length, 55 in. Oak.......... 45 00 Mahogany.......... 70 00
Length, 60 in. Oak.......... 48 00 Mahogany.......... 76 00

No. 8. High roll top. Beveled cross panels. Four long letter files down left side. Full of convenient drawers. Pan tray and ink wells. Large center drawer. Elegant Golden Quartered Oak or Solid Mahogany, piano polish. All sizes are 36 in. deep and 50 in. high.
Length, 50 in. Oak..........$55 00 Mahogany.........$ 75 00
Length, 55 in. Oak.......... 63 00 Mahogany......... 85 00
Length, 60 in. Oak.......... 70 00 Mahogany......... 93 00
Length, 66 in. Oak.......... 80 00 Mahogany......... 105 00

No. 16. Has the same material and the same interior as No. 8, but is 38 inches deep, all arms pilasters, base and top are of thicker material.
Length, 60 in. Oak..........$ 75 00 Mahogany..........$108 00
Length, 66 in. Oak......... 92 50 Mahogany......... 130 00
Length, 72 in. Oak......... 110 00 Mahogany.. .... 152 00

Center column: No. 25; 42 in. $2400, 50 in. $3000, 55 in. $3600, 60 in. $4500. No. 1; 42 in. $3000, 50 in. $3500, 55 in. $3800, 60 in. $4500, 66 in. $5000. No. 125; 50 in. $3500, 55 in. $4000, 60 in. $5000. No. 20; 50 in. $4500, 55 in. $4800, 60 in. .$6500. No. 4; 50 in. $5000, 55 in. $6000, 60 in. $8000.
Right column: No. 13; 50 in. $2400, 55 in. $3000, 60 in. $4000. No. 11; 50 in. $4000, 55 in. $5000, 60 in. $5000. No. 8; 50 in. $5000, 55 in. $6000, 60 in. $7000, 66 in. $8000. No. 16; 60 in. $8000, 66 in. $9000, 72 in. $10,000.

O. C. S. OLSEN & CO.
MANUFACTURERS OF
OFFICE DESKS,
15, 17, 19 AND 21 NORTH CLINTON ST.,
CHICAGO, ILL.

Do You Handle Desks?

If so, kindly compare the values below with what you are buying, before you throw this in the waste basket.

No. 24.
4 FEET LONG, 2 FEET 6 INCHES WIDE.

No. 25.
4 FEET 4 INCHES LONG, 2 FEET 6 INCHES WIDE.

Antique Oak. Has seven drawers in base, two drawers and two corner drawers in pigeonhole case; two extension slides; polished wood writing table; full paneled finished back; front raised bevel paneled; drawers in top part hand carved; lower drawer on right-hand side eleven inches deep inside and partitioned for books; partitions in two upper drawers; combination lock; tongue and groove dust-proof curtain; card rack and letter drop at each end; polish finish.

The Cheapest Complete and Well Made Roll Top Desks in the Market.

PRICE, No. 24............$23.00.
$2500

PRICE, No. 25............$27.00.
$3000

TERMS:
3 per cent. off 30 Days,
5 " " 10 "

No. 34.
4 FEET 4 INCHES LONG, 2 FEET 6 INCHES WIDE.

Antique oak; paneled finished back; covered with imitation leather or cloth.

PRICE, No. 34...$9.60.
$1000

The Details of the Tyler Desks are Finer than any others.—Tyler Desk Co., St. Louis, Mo.

824 CLOSED.   824 OPEN.

No. 824. Tyler's Low Roll Curtain. Antique Oak, Walnut or Cherry.

inches wide, 56 inches long, 43 inches high; our Patented Curtain; Finished and Paneled all around; Extra Fine Fancy Veneer on Front and Ends; Extension
es in Table; Elegantly Carved Posts; Finest Finish; Zinc Bottom; Covered with Billiard Cloth; Casters, &c.   Weight, 250 lbs.   Price, F. O B............ **$70 00**

$5000

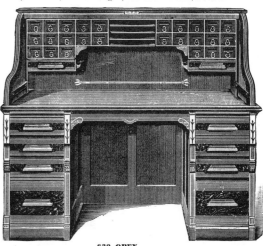

832 CLOSED.   832 OPEN.

No. 832. Tyler's High Roll Curtain. Walnut, Antique Oak or Cherry.

nches wide, 60 inches long, 51 inches high; our Latest Patented Curtain; Built-up and Handsomely Veneered Writing Table; Zinc Bottoms; Closed
red Veneer Panels and Drawer Fronts; Finished all around; Secret Drawers; Lower Drawers Partitioned for Books; Extension Slides in Table;
; Casters, &c.   This desk combines greatest amount of space; largest writing table, convenient internal arrangement, with compactness in size a
sign.   Weight, 275 lbs.   Price, F. O. B.. **$78 00**

$8000

The Tyler Desks are sold in every civilized country on the Globe.—Tyler Desk Co., St. Louis, Mo.

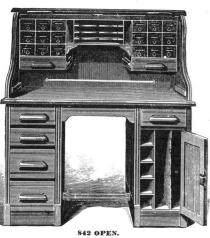

Trade Mark.

This Solid Gilt Plate will be found over front
curtain key hole of all genuine Tyler Roll Top
Desks.

842 OPEN.

**2. Tyler's High Roll Curtain Desk—Walnut, Antique Oak
or Cherry.**

hes wide, 48 inches long, 51 inches high. Our Patented
; Built-up and Handsomely Veneered Writing Table;
Polished; Paneled Ends and Sides; Automatic Lock;
y locks the entire Desk. Files; Brass Rod and Casters
te. Weight, 175 lbs. Price, F. O. B................**$48 00**

$4500

**No. 841. Tyler's High Roll Curtain Desk. Walnut, Antique Oak
or Cherry.**

Size, 30 inches wide, 42 inches long, 51 inches high. Our Built-up
and Handsomely Veneered Writing Table; Highly Polished;
Paneled Ends and Sides; Automatic Lock; One Key unlocks entire Desk. Files; Brass Rod and Casters complete. Weight. 150
lbs. Price, F. O. B.. **$38 00**

$3600

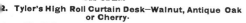

When Cheap Desks are Laid on the Shelf these Desks will be on Duty.—Tyler Desk Co., St. Louis, Mo.

821 CLOSED.   821 OPEN.

No. 821. Tyler's Low Roll Curtain Desk. Walnut, Antique Oak or Cherry.

Size, 32 inches wide, 52 inches long, 43 inches high. Our Patented Curtain; Finished all around; Closed Back; Fine Fancy Veneered Panels; Extension Slides and Table; Extra Finish: Zinc Bottoms; Covered with Billiard Cloth; Mice and Dust Proof; Files; Brass Rod and Casters complete. Weight, 300 lbs. Price, F. O. B.....................................

848 OPEN.   848 CLOSED.

No. 848. Tyler's Extra High Roll Curtain Desk. Walnut, Antique Oak or Cherry.

Size, 34 inches wide, 52 inches long, 66 inches high. Our Patented Curtain; Our Built-up Table and Panels; Plain Back; Veneered Drawer Fronts; Cupboards in Front and Side; Secret Drawers; Automatic Lock. One key unlocks the entire desk. Covered with Felt Cloth, or our Veneered Writing Table; Files; Casters and Brass Rod complete. Weight, 200 lbs. Price, F. O. B.....................................

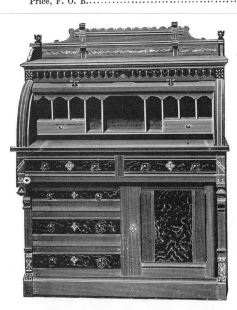

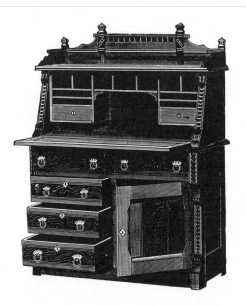

No. 344. Tyler's Walnut, Antique Oak or Cherry Mahogany Finish Cabinet Desk.

Size, 43x26 inches. Very Handsome; French Veneered Panels; Five Drawers and Closet with Shelf; Billiard Cloth Sliding Table. Weight, 90 lbs. Price, F. O. B **$36 00** *$3500*

No. 389. Tyler's Fall Leaf Cabinet. Walnut, Antique Oak or Cherry Mahogany Finish.

Size, 43x19 inches. Very Handsome Doctor's Cabinet. Price, F. O. B.............. **$24 00** *$2400*

No. 339. Tyler's Walnut, Antique Cherry Mahogany Finish Cylinder D

Size, 34x23 inches. Elegant; French Veneered Panels; Billiard Cloth Sliding Table. Weight, 50 lbs. Price, F. O. B

The Heaviest and Finest Desks made in America.—Tyler Desk Co., St. Louis, Mo.

9. Tyler's Automatic Iron Tram, Swing Pedestal, Low Roll Top Desk. Walnut, Antique Oak or Cherry.

Best Swing Corner Desk on Earth. Extra Heavy. Solid. (Government Standard.)
et 8 inches long; 2 feet 8 inches deep. Low Top; Handsome Veneered Front
ers and Revolving Case; have Best Tumbler Locks. For style of back and
closed, see cuts A and B. Files, Brass Rod and Casters complete. Weight,
s. Price, F. O. B.. **$65 00**

$6000

No. 740. Tyler's Automatic Iron Tram, Swing Pedestal, Low Roll Top Desk. Antique Oak, Walnut or Cherry. (Government Standard.)

Size, 4 feet 6 inches long, 2 feet 10 inches deep, 3 feet 7 inches high. Low Top;
Handsome Veneered Front; Drawers Locked by Closing of Curtain; Revolv-
ing Case and Curtain have Best Tumbler Locks; Handsome Raised Panels,
Sides and Back. See cuts A and B. Files, Brass Rod and Casters complete.
Weight, 350 lbs. Price, F. O. B... **$100 00**

$7500

Showing style of Heavy Panel Work in Back and Ends of our Extra Heavy Government Desks, Nos. 739, 740, 741, 742, 743 and 744.

Cut B. Showing Desks Nos. 739, 740, 741, 742, 743 and 744 Closed.
Government Standard Work.

Tyler's Automatic, Iron Tram, Swing Pedestal, Low Roll Curtain Desk. Walnut, Antique Oak or Cherry. (Government Standard.)

long, 3 feet wide, 3 feet 8 inches high. Low Top; Handsome Veneered Front;
locked by closing Curtain; Revolving Case and Curtains have Best Tumbler
Desk Paneled with Heavy, Handsome, Raised Panels on Sides and Back. See cuts
All drawers have adjustable partitions. Best Patent Casters; Files; Brass Rod.
350 lbs. Price, F. O. B............................... **$116 00**

$10,000

No. 742. Tyler's Automatic, Iron Tram, Swing Pedestal Low Roll Curtain Desk. Walnut, Antique Oak or Cherry. (Government Standard.)

Size, 4 feet 6 inches long, 2 feet 10 inches deep, 3 feet 7 inches high. Low Top; Has Two
Revolving Cases; Handsome Veneer Front; Best Tumbler Locks in Cases and Curtain;
Desk Paneled with Heavy, Handsome, Raised Panels on Sides and Back. See cuts A and
B. Best Patent Casters; Rod and Files complete. Weight, 350 lbs. Price, F. O. B **$120 00**

$12,000

See that the Tyler Name Plate is on your Roll Top Desks—Tyler Desk Co., St. Louis, Mo.

816 CLOSED.

816 OPEN.

No. 816. Tyler's Low Roll Curtain Desk—Walnut, Antique Oak or Cherry.

Size, 30 inches wide, 43 inches long, 43 inches high. Our Patented Curtain; Finished Back; Fine Fancy Veneered Panels; Extra Finish; Zinc Bottoms; Covered with Billiard Cloth; Files, Brass Rod and Casters complete. Weight, 125 lbs. Price, F. O. B.....................................$

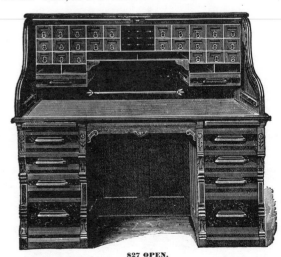

825 CLOSED.

825 OPEN.

No. 825. Tyler's Low Roll Curtain Desk—Walnut, Antique Oak or Cherry.

Size, 26 inches wide, 40 inches long, 41 inches high; Our Patented Curtain; Sliding Table (slides 8 inches); paneled ends and sides; Fancy Ornamental Top; Zinc Bottoms; Covered with Billiard Cloth; Files, Brass Rod and Casters complete. Weight, 125 lbs. Price, F. O. B.................................$

827 CLOSED.

827 OPEN.

No. 827. Tyler's High Roll Curtain. Walnut, Oak or Cherry.

Size, 36 inches wide, 56 inches long, 52 inches high; our Patented Curtain; Zinc Bottoms; Absolutely Dust and Vermin Proof; Paneled and Finished all around; Extra Fine Fancy Veneer on Front and Ends; Elegantly Carved Posts; Extension Slides in Table; Finest Finish; Covered with Billiard Cloth; Casters, &c., complete. Weight, 300 lbs. Price, F. O. B.................................$

CENTRAL MANUFACTURING CO.

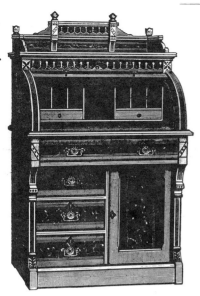

No. 210 CYLINDER DESK.

Size, 34x23 inches.

Walnut, Cherry or Oak, plain back, four drawers, shelf in closet; Billiard Cloth on writing part.

Price—In white, $23.00 ; finished, $27.00.

$2500

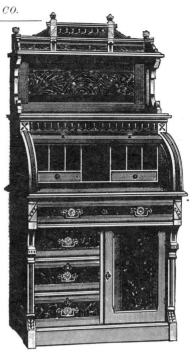

No. 209 CYLINDER DESK.

34x27

Size, ~~42x23~~ inches.

Walnut, Cherry or Oak, plain back, four drawers, shelf in closet; Billiard Cloth on writing part.

Price—In white, $24.00 ; finished, $29.00. *$3000*

No. 214 PARLOR CURTAIN DESK.

Size, 35x22 inches.

Price—In Walnut, Cherry or Oak, in white, $27.00; finished, $31.00. In solid Mahogany, in white, $31.50; finished, $35.00.

$1800

No. 215 LADIES' WRITING DESK.

Size, 29x25 inches.

Walnut, Cherry or Oak, bevel top, finished back, hinged lid; opening under lid arranged with pigeon holes, convenient for stationery, etc.; three drawers in end ; top covered with Billiard Cloth.

Price—In white, $15.00; finished, $18.00.

$1800

BARDWELL, ANDERSON & CO., BOSTON, MASS. FOR THE TRADE ONLY.

No. 84. DESK. Open.

Length, 32 inches; width, 19 inches; height, 3½ feet.

Cylinder top. Cloth covered Slide. Pigeon holes. Four Drawers, locks, and keys.

Walnut, Imitation Mahogany, or Quartered Oak.

$1200

No. 85. DESK. Closed.

Length, 32 inches; width, 20 inches; height, 5 feet.

Cylinder top. Cloth covered Slide. Pigeon holes. Four Drawers, locks, and keys. Paneled Ends.

Walnut, Imitation Mahogany, or Quartered Oak.

No. 223 CURTAIN DESK.

Size, 60x36 inches; 52 inches high.

Walnut, Cherry or Oak, finished back; Billiard Cloth or polished five-ply wood writing part; book-rack in lower right hand drawer; slides above drawers.

Price—In white, $60.00; finished, $70.00.

Pigeon-hole compartment same as shown in No. 222, with a book-rack at each end.

$6000

No. 224 CURTAIN DESK.

Size, 50x30 inches.

Finished back; combination lock on drawers; Billiard Cloth or polished five-ply wood writing part; book-rack in lower right hand drawer; slide above drawers on left hand side.

Price—In Walnut, Cherry or Oak, in white, $40.00; finished, $45.00.

$4000

No. 227 CURTAIN DESK.

Size, 44x30 inches.

Finished back, combination lock on drawers; book-rack in lower drawer; Billiard Cloth or polished five-ply wood writing part.

Price—In Walnut, Cherry or Oak, in white, $31.00; finished, $36.00.

$2500

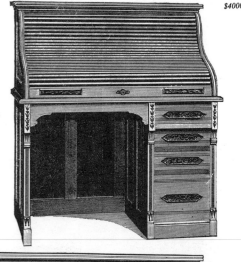

No. 195 CYLINDER DESK.

Size, 43x26 inches.

Walnut, Cherry or Oak, finished back; Billiard Cloth on slide.

Price—In white, $20.00; finished, $24.50.

$1900

No. 228 CURTAIN DESK.

Size, 48x30 inches.

Finished back; Billiard Cloth or polished five-ply wood writing part.

Price—In Walnut, Cherry or Oak, in white, $24.00; finished, $27.00.

$2000

NORTHWESTERN FURNITURE CO., BURLINGTON, IOWA.

No. 380—Class A.

in. long, 34 in. deep, 45 in. high. Made in Walnut, Cherry or Oak.
in either Antique or 16th Century finish. Oak has quartered panels and top. High
sh finish all around. Has 3-ply framed, figured Oak Writing Bed, and one deep
wer has Leopold's (patent applied for) Adjustable Letter File. Four partitioned
wers. Our dust-proof curtain. Oak pigeon hole, ~~with movable boxes, and mirror~~
~~entre~~. All Oak drawers, finished inside.

$4500

No. 381—Class A.

54 in. long, 34 in. deep, 51 in. high. Made in Walnut, Cherry or Oak.
Oak in either Antique or 16th Century finish. Oak has quartered panels and top. High
polish finish all around. Has 3-ply framed, figured Oak Writing Bed, and one deep
drawer has Leopold's (patent applied for) Adjustable Letter File. Four partitioned
drawers. Our dust-proof curtain. Oak pigeon hole, with movable boxes, and mirror
in centre. All Oak drawers, finished inside.

$5000

No. 340—Class B.

in. long, 32 in. deep, 45 in. high. Made in Walnut, Cherry or Oak, high
ish finish all round. Oak in either Antique or 16th Century finish. Has
ly framed, figured Oak Writing Bed, and our improved dust-proof curtain.
ree partitioned drawers.

$2200

No. 351—Class B.

48 in. long, 32 in. deep, 51 in. high. Made in Walnut, Cherry or Oak.
Oak in either 16th Century or Antique finish. Oak has quartered top and
panels. High polish finish all around. Has 3-ply framed, figured Oak
Writing Bed, and our improved dust-proof curtain. Five partitioned drawers.

$3800

NORTHWESTERN FURNITURE CO., Burlington, Iowa.

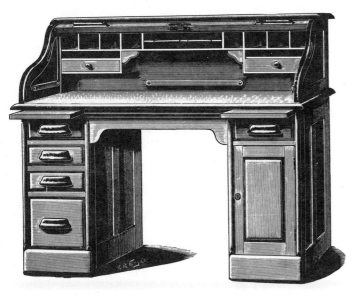

No. 327—Class C.

54 in. long, 32 in. deep, 45 in. high.   Made only in Antique Finished Oak.
Has solid panels and solid quartered Oak Polished Bed.   Three partitioned
drawers.   *$2000*

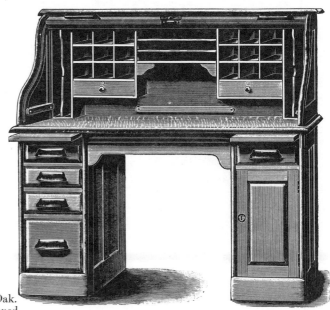

No. 328—Class C.

54 in. long, 32 in. deep, 51 in. high.   Made only in Antique Finished C
Has solid panels and solid quartered Oak Polished Bed.   Three partitio
drawers.   *$2500*

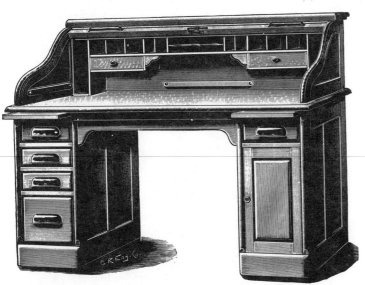

No. 329—Class C.

60 in. long, 32 in. deep, 45 in. high.   Made only in Antique Finished Oak.
Has solid panels and solid quartered Oak Polished Bed.   Three partitioned
drawers.   *$2500*

No. 332—Class C.

42 in. long, 32 in. deep, 45 in. high.   Made in Antique Finished Oak
Has solid panels and solid quartered Oak Polished Bed.   Two partiti
drawers.   *$2000*

PARLOR DESK.

NEW DESIGN.

PARLOR DESK WITH CABINET BOOK CASE.

No. 30.

18 in. deep, 42 in. high, 32 in. wide.

Price, ... $24.00. *$1800*

From selected stock in Antique Oak and Cherry. Spacious writing bed, solid brass handles, escutcheons and hinges. Fine polish finish. Handsomely carved and moulded. No. 31 shows this desk with open writing bed.

No. 31.

Desk same description as No. 30.

Price, ... $32.00. *$2200*

Attractive in appearance; saves space, as two articles of need are combined in one. Just the thing for home use. Can be furnished with brass rod for curtains in place of doors.

Tyler Desk Co., St. Louis, Mo.

No. 3185. Tyler's Little Gem. Walnut, Cherry or Oak.

ze, 6 ft. 11 in. high by 3 ft. wide. 3 Drawers, Sliding Table, &c. A Cylinder Secretary especially adapted to young Ladies, Doctors, or House use. Casters Fitted. Weight 150 lbs. Portable. Shipped K. D. Price, F. O. B........**$36 00**
$4000

No. 306½. Tyler's Walnut, Antique Oak or Cherry Cylinder Secretary.

Size, 42x25 in. 8 ft. 4 in. high; French Glass, 14x34 in., French Veneered Panels; Adjustable Shelves in Top Case; Billiard Cloth on Writing Table; Portable; Shipped K. D. Weight, 175 lbs. Price, F. O. B................**$42 50**
$5000

No. 388. Tyler's Walnut, Antique Oak or Cherry Fall Leaf Secretary.

Size, 44x19 in., 7 ft. 10 in. high; Fench Glass, 16x32 in., French Veneered Panels; Adjustable Shelves in Top Case; Portable; Shipped K. D. Weight, 200 lbs. Price, F. O. B..... **$38 00**
$4500

Tyler Desk Co., St. Louis, Mo.

No. 395. Tyler's Parlor Cabinet Desk. Walnut, Antique Oak or Cherry Mahogany Finish.

Size, 30x18 inches. Writing Part Covered with Billiard Cloth; Portable. Price, F. O. B............................ **$20 00**

$2200

No. 348. Tyler's Fancy Parlor Desk. Walnut, Antique Oak or Cherry.

Size, 34x23 inches. Sliding Table; Ornamental Shelf on Top; Billiard Cloth on Slide; Elegantly Veneered. Guaranteed to please any one. Weight, 100 lbs. Price, F. O. B...................... **$30 00**

$3000

No. 396. Tyler's Parlor Cabinet Desk. Walnut, Antique Oak or Cherry Mahogany Finish.

Size, 30x18 inches. Writing Part Covered with Billiard Cloth. If desired, will put Mirror in Back, in place of Veneered Panels, at same price. Portable. Price, F. O. B............................ **$25**

$250

No. 307. Walnut, Antique Oak or Cherry Cylinder Secretary.

Size, extreme width, 48x26 in., 8 ft. 6 in. high. French Glass, 16x36 in. French Veneered Panels; Four Drawers; Book Closet on the right; Shelf in Closet on the left; Adjustable Shelves in Top Case; Billiard Cloth on Slide. Handsomest made. Portable. Shipped K. D. Same when open as No. 352½. Weight 225 lbs. Price, F O. B.. **$65 00**

$5500

No. 352½. Tyler's Walnut, Antique Oak or Cherry Mahogany Finish Cylinder Secretary.

Size, 45x26 in., 8 ft. 6 in. high. French Veneered Panels; Five Drawers and Closet with Shelf in Base; Double Doors in Top; French Glass, 16x34 in.; Adjustable Shelves; Billiard Cloth on Slide; Heavy Carved Top; Combination Base; Casters Complete. Portable. Shipped K. D. Pin Hinges and Dust Proof. Same when closed as No. 307. Weight 200 lbs. Price, F. O. B..................... .....**$55 00**

$6000

No. 91½. DESK, or SECRETARY.

Length, 32 inches; width, 18 inches; height, 7½ feet.
The Base of this Secretary is the same Desk as that described on the opposite page.

Walnut, Imitation Mahogany, or Quartered Oak.

$2500

No. 85½. DESK, or SECRETARY. Closed.

Length, 32 inches; width, 20 inches; height, 6¾ feet.

The Base of this Secretary is the same Desk as that described on pages 74 and 75.

Walnut, Imitation Mahogany, or Quartered Oak.

$3000

Tyler Desk Co., St. Louis, Mo.

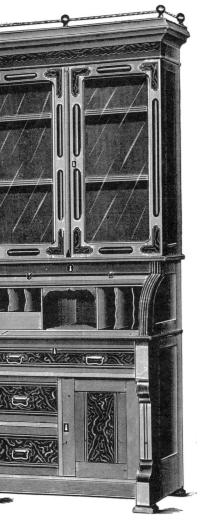

186. Tyler's Fancy Rail Combination Base Secretary. Walnut, Oak or Cherry.

...t 10 inches high, 3 feet wide. Fancy through— Sliding Table, etc. Casters Fitted. Portable. ...ped K. D. Weight 175 lbs. Price, F. O. B., **$43 00**

$4000

No. 3154. Tyler's New Cable Secretary. Walnut, Oak or Cherry.

Size, 7 ft. 8 in. high, 3 ft. 6 in. wide. A beautiful Design and the Handsomest Combination Base Secretary made. Casters Fitted. Portable. Shipped K. D. Weight 200 lbs. Price, F. O. B.................**$44 00**

$5000

No. 3142. Tyler's 3-Drawer Cylinder Secretary. Walnut or Cherry.

Size, 7 ft. 9 in. high, 3 ft. 5½ wide. Sliding Table, covered with Billiard Cloth. Casters Fitted. Portable. Shipped K. D. Weight 200 lbs. Price, F. O. B....**$38 50**

$4500

No. 242 FALL LEAF SECRETARY.

Size, 44x19 inches; 7 feet 10 inches high.

Double French glass, 16x32 inches; adjustable shelves in top case.

Price—In Walnut, Cherry or Oak, in white, $27.00; finished, $33.00.

$3600

No. 248 CYLINDER SECRETARY.

Size, 36x23 inches; 7 feet 10 inches high.
Double thick French glass, 12x36.

Price—In Walnut, Cherry or Oak, in white, $29.00; finished, $36.00.

No. 247. The same with three full-width drawers in base, same price.

$4500

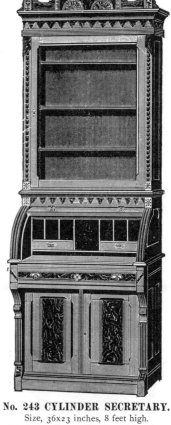

No. 243 CYLINDER SECRETARY.

Size, 36x23 inches, 8 feet high.
Single door, adjustable shelves in top, double thick French glass, size
Billiard Cloth on slide.

Price—In Walnut, Cherry or Oak, in white, $27.00; finished, $34

No: 244.
The same, with three full-width drawers below; in white, $29; finish

$4200

No. 249 CYLINDER SECRETARY.

Size, 42x 25 inches; 8 feet high.

Double thick French glass 14x34 inches, adjustable shelves in top case;
Billiard Cloth on slide.

Price—In Walnut, Cherry or Oak, in white, $32.00; finished, $38.00.

$5000

No. 207.
Walnut with Maple ends, and Antique Oak.
3 ft. 2 in. wide, 7 ft. 2 in. high.

$3000

No. 263.
Walnut and Antique Oak.   3 ft. 3 in. wide, 7 ft. 7 in. high.
Glass, 15x32.

$4300

No. 261.
Walnut and Antique Oak.   2 ft. 10 in. wide, 7 ft. 2 in. high.

$4000

No. 266.
Antique Oak.   3 ft. 3 in. wide, 7 ft. 7 in. high.
Glass, 15x32.

$4000

No. 267.
Walnut and Antique Oak.   2 ft. 10 in. wide, 7 ft. 4 in. high.
French burl veneers on walnut cases.

$4000

No. 270.
Walnut and Antique Oak.   3 ft. 4 in. wide, 7 ft. 8 in. high.
Glass, 15x32.   French burl veneers on walnut cases.

$5000

ROCKFORD UNION FURNITURE COMPANY.   ROCKFORD, ILLINOIS.

No. 12 BOOKCASE.—Closed.

Antique Oak or XVI. century; 3 ft. 2 in. wide, 6 ft. 10 in. high.

$2500

No. 13 BOOKCASE.—Open.

Antique Oak or XVI. century; 3 ft. 2 in. wide, 6 ft. 10 in. high.

$2800

No. 18 CYLINDER CASE.

Antique Oak or XVI. century; 3 ft 3 in. wide, 7 ft. 8 in. high.

$4000

No. 19 COMBINATION CYLINDER.

Antique Oak or XVI. century; 3 ft. 3 in. wide, 7 ft. 8 in. high.

$4500

No. 20 ROLLER CYLINDER.

Antique Oak or XVI. century; 3 ft. 10 in. wide, 8 ft. high. For closed see No. 21.

$4800

No. 21 DESK.

Antique Oak or XVI. century; 3 ft. 10 in. wide. For inside see No. 20.

The lock that closes the roller front locks all the drawers. The best Desk on the market for the money.
Give us a sample order.

$4500

STICKLEY-BRANDT FURNITURE CO., BINGHAMTON, N. Y.

No. 394. Book-Case and Writing Desk Combined, 5 ft. 2 in. high, 37 in. wide, Solid Golden Oak, French bevel mirror 14x6.
Price...................................$11.90
$1200

No. 403. Book-Case and Writing Desk Combined, 5 ft. 6 in. high, 40 in. wide. French bevel mirror 18x12. Golden Quartered Oak.
Price...................................$17.90
$1200

No. 392. Book-Case and Writing Desk Combined, Golden Quartered Oak, 40 in. wide, 68 in. high, French bevel mirror 10x17, bent glass in door.
Price...................................$18.90
$1500

No. 400. Book-Case and Writing Desk Combined, Golden Quartered Oak, polish finish, 5 ft. 8 in. high, 40 in. wide, adjustable shelves, pattern French bevel mirror 12x16.
Price...................................$18.75
$1500

No. 684. Book-Case and Writing Desk Combined, Golden Quartered Oak, 36 in. wide, 7 feet high.
Price...................................$19.85
$1200

No. 393. Book-Case and Writing Desk Combined, Golden Quartered Oak, 40 in. wide, 68 in. high. French bevel mirror 10x17, bent glass door.
Price...................................$19.85
$1400

No. 391. Book-Case and Writing Desk Combined, 68 in. high, 42 in. wide, pattern French bevel mirror 16x12, Golden Quartered Oak.
Price...................................$21.00
$1400

No. 396. Book-Case and Writing Desk Combined, Golden Quartered Oak, 44 in. wide, 70 in. high, French bevel mirror 14x16.
Price...................................$24.50
$1400

No. 796. Book-Case and Writing Desk Combined, 6 ft. 3 in. high, 46 in. wide. Golden Quartered Oak, piano polish. Full serpentine front and glass door, pattern French bevel mirror 18x18.
Price...................................$37.50
$1200

No. 33.

16½ in. deep, 46 in. wide, 60 in. high.

Price, ... $55.00

Parlor Desk, Book Case and Cabinet combined, three in one. The best of all combinations at a low price. Made from best selected stock in old Oak and Cherry. Every inch of space utilized. Heavy bevel French mirror, polished brass lever to support writing

$2200

No. 289 Cabinet Bookcase. (Open.)

Oak, Antique, Polished Finish. Height, 6 ft. 3 in.; width, 3 ft. 4 in.
Glass, 14x28; French bevel plate mirror, 16x14.

$2800

No. 290 Cabinet Bookcase. (Open.)

Oak, Polished Finish, Antique or XVIth Century Oxidized Brass Trimmings. With or
without French bevel mirror in door over desk. Height, 6 ft. 6 in.;
width, 4 ft. 6 in. Glass, 16x26 and 16x21.

$3500

No. 306 Cabinet Bookcase. (Open.)

Oak, Polished Finish, Antique or XVIth Century. Height, 6 ft. 2 in.; width 5 ft. 6 in. Glass,
14x48, 8x16 in small doors over desk.

$4500

No. 303 Cabinet Bookcase. (Open.)

Oak, Antique or XVIth Century, Polished Finish. Height, 5 ft. 10 in.; width, 3 ft. 10 in.
Glass 16x42; French bevel plate mirrors in top doors, 9x19.

$2600

Tyler Desk Co., St. Louis, Mo.

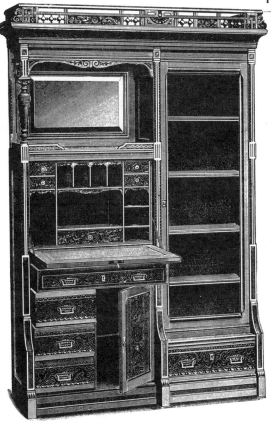

No. 390. Tyler's Library Secretary. Mahoganized Cherry. Antique Oak or Walnut.

4 ft. 3 in. wide, 6 ft. 3 in. high; Bevel French Plate above Desk, size 12x20; Glass in Door, 16x48; Adjustable Shelves. This is the Handsomest made. Weight, 200 lbs. Price, F. O. B.................$68 00

$3800

No. 392. Tyler's Three-Section Library Secretary. Very Fine Walnut, Antique Oak or Cherry Mahogany Finish.

Size, 5 feet 9 inches wide, 6 feet 6 inches high. Fall Leaf Secretary, 25 inches wide; Writing Part covered with Billiard Cloth; French Glass in Doors, size 12x50 inches; Adjustable Shelves; Portable; Shipped K. D.; Weight 250 lbs.

Price, F. O. B $75 00

$4800

ROCKFORD UNION FURNITURE COMPANY.

ROCKFORD, ILLINOIS.

No. 500 LIBRARY.—Open.

Antique Oak or XVI. century; 3 ft. 10 in. wide, 6 ft. 2 in. high.

$2800

No. 501 LIBRARY.—Closed.

Antique Oak or XVI. century; 3 ft. 8 in. wide, 6 ft. 3 in. high; French bevel plate 14x14.

$4000

No. 503 LIBRARY.—Open.

Antique Oak or XVI. century ; 3 ft. 8 in. wide, 6 ft. high ; French bevel plate 12x18.
Best Case in America for the money. Give us sample order.

$4500

No. 511 LIBRARY.—Open.

Antique Oak or XVI. century ; 3 ft. 8 in. wide, 6 ft. high ; French plate 14x14 ; bookcase glass 18x

$4000

C. & A. KREIMER CO.
BOOKCASES.

No. 26—Walnut.

Height, 6 ft. 9 in.   Width, 4 ft. 2 in.
No. 26½—China Case.   Same as above, but 4 in. deeper.

$3600

No. 25—Walnut and Oak.

Height, 6 ft. 6 in.   Width, 4 ft. 6 in.

$4000

Bookcases

No. 410. Tyler's Dwarf Book Case. Walnut, Antique Oak or Cherry.

5 ft. 6 in. high, 3 ft. 4 in. wide, 13 in. deep; Adjustable Shelves; Brass Pole and Rings. Rub Finish and Polished. Weight, 125 lbs. Price, F. O. B.. $18 00

$950

CENTRAL MANUFACTURING CO.

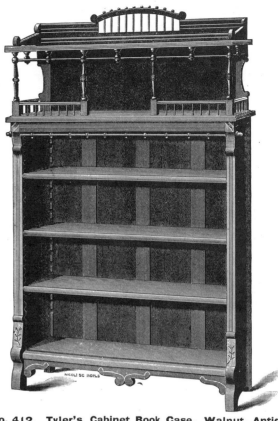

No. 412. Tyler's Cabinet Book Case. Walnut, Antique Oak or Cherry.

Size, 5 ft. high, 3 ft. 4 in. wide, 13 in. deep; Adjustable Shelves; Brass Pole and Rings for Curtain. Polished. Weight, 140 lbs. Price, F. O. B...... .... $20 00

$1500

No. 263 OPEN BOOK CASE.

Size, 3 feet 6 inches wide, 5 feet high.

Adjustable shelves; brass curtain pole and rings,

or leather trimmings on shelves.

Price—In Walnut, Cherry or Oak, in white, $10.00; finished, $12.00.

No. 264.

Same as No. 264. Size, 3 feet wide, 5 feet high.

Price—In white, $9.00; finished, $10.50.

$900

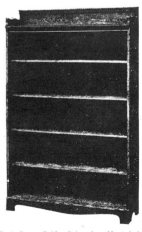

No. 928. Book-Case. Golden Oak, 40 in. wide, 62 in high. Price...$ 8.75
No. 926. Same, 36 in wide. Price........................... 7.25
No. 927. Same, with 2 glass doors, 40 in. wide, 62 in. high. Price... 11.90
No. 925. Same, 1 glass door, 36 in. wide. Price........ .... 9.90
No. 929. Same, 1 glass door, 30 in. wide. Price........... 8.50

No. 928; $700, No. 926; $600, No. 927; $1000, No. 925; $800, No. 929; $700.

No. 265 LIBRARY BOOK CASE.

Size, 4 feet wide, 7 feet 7 inches high.

Double thick French glass, 18x28 inches; adjustable shelves.

Price—In Walnut, Cherry or Oak, in white, $28.00; finished, $36.00.

$1800

No. 268 LIBRARY BOOK CASE.

Size, 4 feet 3 inches wide, 6 feet 3 inches high.

Double thick French glass, 48x18; adjustable shelves.

Price—In Walnut, Cherry or Oak, in white, $28.00; finished, $36.00.

$1950

No. 260 DWARF BOOK CASE.

Size, 5 feet 9 inches high, 3 feet wide.

Double thick French glass, size 24x40; adjustable shelves.

Price—In Walnut, Cherry or Oak, white, $15.00; finished, $21.00.

$1500

No. 261 DWARF BOOK CASE.

Size, 5 feet 8 inches high, 3 feet 6 inches wide.

Double thick French glass size, 14x40; adjustable shelv

Price—In Walnut, Cherry or Oak in white, $20.00; finished,

$1850

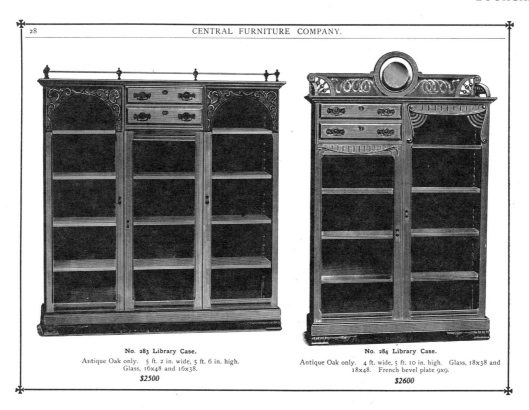

No. 283 Library Case.

Antique Oak only.   5 ft. 2 in. wide, 5 ft. 6 in. high.
Glass, 16x48 and 16x38.

$2500

No. 284 Library Case.

Antique Oak only.   4 ft. wide, 5 ft. 10 in. high.   Glass, 18x38 and
18x48.   French bevel plate 9x9.

$2600

CENTRAL MANUFACTURING CO.

No. 271 LIBRARY BOOK CASE.

Size, 6 feet wide, 7 feet 8 inches high,

Double thick French glass, 60x20 and 60x16; adjustable shelves.

Price—In Walnut, Cherry or Oak, in white, $59.00; finished, $70.00.

$3000

CENTRAL MANUFACTURING CO.

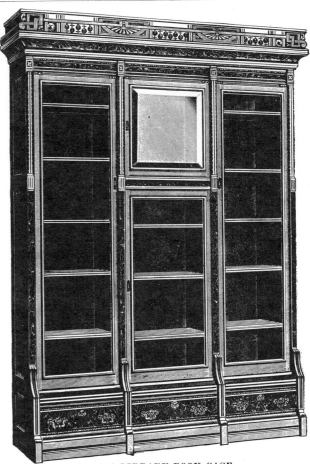

No. 272 LIBRARY BOOK CASE.

Size, 5 feet 3½ inches wide, 7 feet 1½ inches high.

French bevel plate mirror in top center cabinet, 16x16 inches; double thick
French glass in doors, 56x14 and 34x16 inches; adjustable shelves.

Price—In Walnut, Cherry or Oak, in white, $38.00; finished, $50.00.

$4500

No. 286 Library.
Oak. 5 ft. high, 4 ft. wide. Glass, 18x48.
$1500

No. 285 Library.
Oak. 6 ft. high, 4 ft. wide. Glass, 18x38 and 18x48.
$2500

Please examine the details of these Cases; there is nothing better made.—Tyler Desk Co., St. Louis, Mo.

No. 702. Tyler's A Grade Book Case. Made in Walnut only.

Size, 7 feet 10 inches high by 3 feet 8 inches wide, 11 inches deep, Panel Back, Portable, Carved and Veneered, Casters complete. Absolutely first-class in every respect. Shipped K. D., Weight 175 lbs.

Price, F. O. B **$40 00**

$2500

No. 703. Tyler's A Grade Book Case. Walnut or Cherry.

ONE OF THE FINEST CASES MADE.

Height, 8 feet 8 inches, width, 4 feet 6 in. Strictly Portable, Panel Back, very handsomely Carved and Veneered, Casters complete. Shipped K. D. Weight, 200 lbs.

Price, F. O. B **$45 00**

$3000

No. 706½. Tyler's A Grade Extra Deep Case. Made in Walnut only.

8 feet 8 inches high by 4 feet 6 inches wide and 1 Shelves. Nothing finer made. Portable, C complete, Solid Paneled Back. Weight, 200

Price, F. O. B **$5**

Dressers

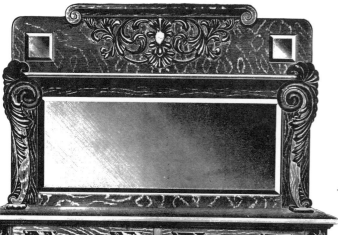

No. 165.—French Bevel Glass. 20x52, 6x6 inches.
5 feet 6 inches wide, 6 feet 7 inches high. One Drawer Lined.
Finished Inside. Oak. $2000

No. 160½.—German Bevel Glass. 18x36 inches. $1800
French " " 6x6 inches.
4 feet wide, 6 feet 8 inches high. One Drawer Lined. 18x36 French Bevel, $2.00 extra.
Oak and Walnut.

No. 167.—German Bevel Glass. 16x28 inches.
3 feet 6 inches wide, 6 feet 6 inches high. One Drawer Lined. Oak.

$1500

No. 164.—French Bevel Glass. 20x46 inches.
5 feet wide, 6 feet 7 inches high. One Drawer Lined.
Finished Inside. Oak.

$2000

Beds and Wardrobes

WARDROBES.

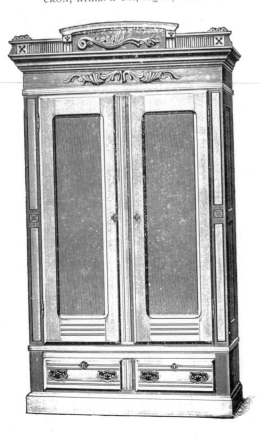

CRIB BED.

No. 7.—Child's Crib Bed. Oak only.
Size, 28x48 inches. One Side Hinged. Fine Antique Trimmings.
These small Beds are very desirable, and sell readily.
54 inch Rails if desired.

$1200

CRON, KILLS & CO., PIQUA, OHIO.

No. 13—Walnut and Oak.

Height, 8 ft. 2 in.   Width 4 ft. 6 in.   Glass, 14 x 54.

$3500

No. 75.   Wardrobe,   -   -   Walnut.
No. 76.   Wardrobe,   -   -   Maple, Imitation Mahogany.
No. 77.   Wardrobe,   -   -   Oak, Antique.

Portable.   Oil Finish.

Height, 7 feet 6 in.   Width, 4 feet 3 in.   Depth, 1 foot 6 in.

$2500

Some American Oak Furniture Sources

The manufacturers and/or retail firms handling oak furniture which were found in the course of researching this subject are listed below. This group is not a complete list of the firms that made and sold oak furniture in America. It is presented merely as an aid for others to build upon.

Allegan Furniture Shops
Allegan, MI

Archer Manufacturing Co.
5, 7 & 9 North Water Street
Rochester, NY
ca. 1885-1890

B. A. Atkinson & Co.
Boston & Portland

Baker Furniture Factories
Allegan, MI

Bardwell, Anderson & Co.
19 Charlestown Street
Boston, MA
ca. 1884-1890

Basic Furniture Co.
Waynesboro, VA

Bassett, J. D. Manufacturing Co.
Bassett, VA

Batesville Cabinet Co.
Batesville, IN

Bentley & Gerwig Furniture Co.
Parkersburg, W. VA.
samples in stock at:
Frederick Goll
195 Canal Street
New York, NY
ca. 1891
manufacturers of antique oak & sixteenth century chamber suits

Berkey & Gay
Grand Rapids, MI

Central Furniture Co.
Rockford, IL
est. 1879
specialties included combination bookcases and cylinder bookcases

Central Manufacturing Co.
37, 39 and 41 Armour Street
Chicago, IL
ca. 1880-1890

Century Furniture Co.
Grand Rapids, MI

Charlotte Furniture Co.
Charlotte, MI

Chicago Desk Manufacturing Co.
Kinzie & Peorie Streets
ca. 1890

Originally organized by Skelvig and Peterson on Clinton Street.

Chittenden & Eastman
Burlington, IW

Clark Bros. & Co.

Clark & Ranney

Colie & Son
284 to 290 Pearl Street
Buffalo, NY
est. 1866
Patent rocking chairs, center tables, parlor furniture

Colonial Desk Co.
Rockford, IL

Cooper & McKee
113, 115, 117 & 119 Gwinnett Street
Brooklyn, NY

Cortland Furniture Co.
Cortland, NY

Cron, Kills & Co.
Piqua, OH

Daniels, Badger & Co.
25 Sudbury and 130 Friend Streets
Boston, MA
ca. 1876-1881

Danner, John
Canton, Ohio
ca. 1886

Derby & Kilmer Desk Co.
93 Causeway Street
Boston, MA
ca. 1885
Factory in Somerville, MA

Elbert Furniture Co.
Red Lion, PA
Founded 1854

Empire Furniture Co.
Rockford, IL

Erskine-Danforth Co.
New York, NY

Excelsior Furniture Co.
Rockford, IL
organized in 1881
upholstered furniture

Fogler, P. M. & Co.
No. 9 Granite Block
Bangor, ME

Forest City Furniture Company
Rockford, IL
founded by A. C. Johnson in 1870.
Employed 300 people by 1889.
Branch established in New York City.

French, William A. Furniture Co.
Minneapolis, MN

Glascock Bros. Manufacturing Co.
Muncie, IN

Globe-Wernicke
Cincinnati, OH

Grand Rapids Bookcase & Chair Co.
Grand Rapids, MI

Grand Rapids Chair Co.
Grand Rapids, MI

Grand Rapids Furniture Co.

Great North Chair Co.
Chicago, IL

Hale & Kilburn Manufacturing Co.
48 & 50 North Sixth Street
Philadelphia, PA
founded in 1867 as Hale, Moseley, Goodman & Co., a looking glass and picture manufacturer. Became Hale & Kilburn in 1873, and began to manufactur furniture.

Hall & Stephen
200, 202 & 204 Canal Street
185 Sixth Avenue
New York, NY
ca. 1882

The Hartley Reclining Chair Company
153 and 155 Superior Street
Chicago, IL
ca. 1885

Hastings Table Co.
Hastings, MI

Hayes Chair Co.
Cortland, NY
ca. 1882

Haywood, W. Chair Co.
442 Pearl Street
New York, NY
ca. 1883

Heller, W. C. & Co.
Montpelier, OH

Henshaw, George
171 Canal Street
New York, NY

Heyman, George
103 & 105 Mott Street
New York, NY
ca. 1890

The Hoosier Manufacturing Co.
28 Ashton Street
New Castle, IN

Imperial Table Co.
Grand Rapids, MI

Indianapolis Cabinet Works
ca. 1888

Ingram Richardson Co.
Frankfort, IN
Hoosier Cabinets

Johnson Furniture Co.
Grand Rapids, MI

Johnson-Handley-Johnson
Grand Rapids, MI

Johnson & Houck
Charlotte, MI
walnut chamber suits
"cheap chamber suits"

Karpen, S. & Bros.
205 East Lake Street
Chicago, IL
est. 1881
parlor furniture by 1886, brothers Sal
and Oscar Karpen were active

Kehr, Peter
123-135 Mangin Street
New York, NY ca. 1882

Keller Sturm & Co.
corner Elizabeth and Fulton Streets
Chicago, IL
ca. 1883

Keller, Sturm & Ehman
corner Elizabeth & Fulton Streets
Chicago, IL
ca. 1885

Kensington Manufacturing Co.
New York, NY

Kent Furniture Manufacturing Co.
Grand Rapids, MI
ca. 1883-1888

Kiel Manufacturing Co.
Manufacturers of Tables
Kiel, WI
Made cabinets for Atwater-Kent
radios as well

Kilborn Whitman & Co.
34 Canal Street
Boston, MA
ca. 1880
also an ad w/ a 46 Canal Street
address

Kittinger Furniture Co.
Buffalo, NY

Knetchel Furniture Co.
Hanover, Ontario, Canada

Kreimer, C. & A.Co.
Southeast corner of Richmond and
Carr Streets
Cincinnati, OH
ca. 1888

Larkin Soap Company
Buffalo, New York
not a manufacturer, but name now
associated with chair styles which
were premium prizes

Leavens, G. M. & Son
34 Canal Street
Boston, MA

Leominster Furniture Mfg. Co.
Leominster, MA

ca. 1882
Limbert, Charles P. Furniture Co.
Grand Rapids & Holland, MI

Luce Furniture Co.
Grand Rapids, MI

The Macey Co.
Grand Rapids, MI

Mahoney, E. H.
96 Cross Street
Boston, MA
ca. 1880-1888
the celebrated Morgan chair with
four reclining positions and reversible
cushions, "The Most Practical,
Comfortable, and Common-sense
Chair Made."

Marks Adjustable Folding Chair Co.
930 Broadway
New York, NY
ca. 1887

Mallette & Raymond Manufacturing
Co.
329 to 333 South Canal Street
Chicago, IL
ca. 1887

Michigan Chair Co.
803 Godfrey Avenue
Grand Rapids, MI
Division of Luce Furniture Shops

Moore Desk Co.
84 East Market Street
Indianapolis, IN
ca. 1888

National Chair Manufacturing Co.
Elbridge, NY
ca. 1888
E. W. Clark & W. C. Ranney,
proprietors

New England Furniture Co.
Grand Rapids, MI
ca. 1890

New Haven Folding Chair Co.
552 State Street
New Haven, CT
ca. 1881
Invalid rolling chairs

Northwestern Furniture Co.
Burlington, IW
ca. 1890

O.C.S. Olsen & Company
15, 17, 19 & 21 North Clinton Street
Chicago, IL

Oriel Cabinet Co.
Grand Rapids, MI
ca. 1885
Fine cabinets

Orpin Bros. & Pond

Ott Lounge Company
93, 95 and 97 Dayton Street
Chicago, IL

1890
Ottowa Furniture Co.
Holland, MI

Peterson, A. & Co.
15—21 Armour Street
Chicago, IL
ca. 1890
The "Hafgar" Patent Desk

Phoenix Furniture Co.
Grand Rapids, MI
branches in Chicago and New York
succeeded Phoenix Manufacturing
Co. in 1872 and founded by William
Berkey. By 1886 the factory was one
of the largest and most complete.

Phoenix Chair Co.
Sheboygan, WI
"Busy Since 1875"

Pierce, E. F.
160 & 162 North Street
Boston, MA
ca. 1875

Pond Desk Company
152 Charleston Street
Boston, MA

Princess Dressing Case Co.
corner of Canal & Bridge Streets
Grand Rapids, MI
ca. 1880

Richter Furniture Co.
New York, NY

Ring, Merrill & Tillotson
Saginaw, MI
selling agents:
Klingman & Limbert
Grand Rapids, MI

Rockford Cabinet Co.
307 Tile Street
Rockford, IL

Rockford Union Furniture Company
Rockford, IL
1890

Royal Furniture Co.
Grand Rapids, MI

Roycroft Shop
East Aurora, NY
ca. 1895
a colony for artisans founded by
Elbert Hubbard in 1895, Arts and
Crafts Movement

Saginaw Furniture Shops
Saginaw, MI

St. Johns Table Co.
Cadillac, MI

Samuels, M. & Co.
164 Mott Street
New York, NY
ca. 1890

Schrenkeisen, M. & H.
23—29 Elizabeth Street

New York, NY
1885

Sellers Company
Elwood, IN

Shaw, Applin & Co.
27 Sudbury Street & 69 Portland
Street
Boston, MA
ca. 1879-1882
(successors to Braman, Shaw & Co.)

Shelbyville Desk Co.
Shelbyville, IN

Shower Brothers Co.
Bloomington, IN
Founded in 1868

Silver Creek Upholstering Co.
Silver Creek, NY

Skandia Furniture Co.
Rockford, IL

Small, S. C. & Co.
71 & 73 Portland Street
Boston, MA
ca. 1886-1888

Steinman & Meyer Furniture Co.
560, 562, 564 & 566 West Sixth Street
Cincinnati, OH
ca. 1880

Stickley Brothers (L. & J. G.)
Grand Rapids, MI
marketed mission furniture under
the name of "Hancraft" younger
brothers of Gustav Stickley

Stickly-Brandt Furniture Company
Binghamton, NY
ca. 1902

Stickley, Gustav
Eastwood, NY
1890's

Stomps Burkhardt Co.
Dayton, OH

Strassel, J. L. Co.
Louisville, Ky

Stuart, F. E.
93—101 Fulton Street
Boston, MA
ca. 1880

Squires Sofa & Cabinet Beds

Taylor Chair Co.
Bedford, OH
ca. 1888
Charles A. Wear was their agent in
that year succeeded William O.
Taylor & Son

Thompson, Perley & Waite
Baldwinville, MA
Warerooms, 84 North Street
Boston, MA

Tyler Desk Co.
500 to 502 North 4th Street
St. Louis, MO
listed in St. Louis, MO directories
from 1884-1892

Union Furniture Co.
ca. 1876

Vaill, E. W. Chair Co.
Worcester, MA
ca. 1879-1881

Wait Chair Co.

Wasmuth Endicott Co.
Andrews, IN
Hoosier cabinets

Weir Co.
Monroe, MI

White, Frank W.
269 Canal Street
New York, NY
ca. 1870

Whitney, O. & Co.
Winchenden, MA

Whittle, Charles P.
35 Fulton Street
Boston, MA

Windsor Folding Bed Co.
Chicago, IL
ca. 1890

Winneberger
252 South 3rd Street
Philadelphia, PA

Wooten Desk Co.
Indianapolis, IN
ca. 1876

Picture Credits

The photographs were taken by Christopher Biondi except where noted by an asterisk (★) in which cases they were supplied by the owners. The following sources are noted: Oak House Antiques, Patascala, Ohio—front cover chair, 4, 5A, B, 8B, C, D, F, 9B, C, E, F, 12A, B, C, D, 13A, B, C, D, 16A, B, C, 17C, D, 18A, 19A, B, 20A, B, C, D, 21A, B, 22C, D, 28C, 30B, C, 31C, 32A, 34D, 35B, C, 36A, B, 37A, C, D, 38A, B, C, D, 39A, C, D, 40B, C, D, 41A, B, C, 42B, C, 43B, 44A, 46A, B, 47A, 48A, C, 49B, 51C, 52A, B, C, 53A, B, 54A, B, C, D, 57A, B, C, D, 58C, 59A, B, C, D, E, 60A, B, 61A, B, C, 62A, B, C, D, 63B, C, 64A, 65A, 66A, B, C, 67C, 68B, 69A, B, C, 70A, B, C, D, E, 71A, B, C, D, E, 72C, D, E, F, 73A, B, 74C, D, 75B, C, D, 76A, B, C, D, 77C, D, 78A, B, C, 79A, 80A, C, 81C, 82B, C, 83A, 84A, D, 85A, B, 88A, B, C, 96A, B, C, 97B, C, 98A, B, C, 99B, 101D, 102A, B, D, 103B, D, 104A, B, C, D, 105A, C, 106A, B, C, E, 107A, B, C, 108B, C, 109B, C, D, 110A, 111A, B, 112B. Southwood Antiques, Dallastown, Pennsylvania—title page, 8A, 17A, B, 18B, C, 22A, B, 23A, B, C, 24A, B, C, D, 25A, B, C, 26B, 27A, B, 28A, B, C, 29A, B, C, 30A, 31B, 32B, 33B, 34A, B, C, 37B, 39B, 42A, 45B, 48B, 49A, 50A, B, 55C, 56A, B, 67A, 72A, 73C 74A, 75A, 77A, 80B, 81A, 82A, 83C, 84C, 86A, B, 87A, B, 88D, 89A, B, C, D, 90A, B, C, 93A, B, C, 94A, B, C, 95A, B, C, 99A, C, 100B, 101A, 102C, 103A, 103C, 110B, 112A. Stevens Antiques, Frazer, Pennsylvania—8E, 9A, D, 26A, 27D, 31A★, 33A★, C★, 35A★, 40A, 43A★, C★, 44B, 45A★, 51A★, B★, 54E, 55A★, B★, 56C★, D★, 58A★, B, 63A, 65B, 67B, 68A, 68C, 72B, 74B★, 77B★, 79B★, C, D, 81B, 83B, 84B, 91A, B, C, 92A, B, C, 97A★, 100C, D★, 101B★, C★, 105B★, 108A, 109A★, 111C★, 112C.

Related Books from Schiffer Publishing

Antique Wicker From the Heywood - Wakefield Catalog. Heywood-Wakefield Co. furnished countless American homes with household and outdoor furniture, particularly chairs, for over a century. This is the largest catalog of the pre-eminent wicker and wood furniture manufacturer from the peak of wicker's popularity in the 1920s, presenting 925 examples of Heywood-Wakefield Co. furniture in one volume, including chairs, sofas, beds, tables, bird cages, planters, desks, wardrobes, suites and childrens furniture.
Size: 11" x 8 1/2"   Price Guide   60 pp.
925 pieces illustrated
ISBN: 0-88740-618-1   soft cover $19.95

The Cabinetmakers of America Ethel Hall Bjerkoe. This book lists 2500 American cabinetmakers with biographies, dates, and locations. Numerous beautiful illustrations, photographs, line drawings, and the glossary help to define the furniture.
Size: 7" x 10"   122 photos/drawings   272 pp.
Index
ISBN: 0-916838-14-5   hard cover $22.50

Country Furniture and Accessories from Quebec Warren I. Johansson. A guide to the sources and kinds of Quebec country antiques currently in the United States. It presents a brief history of the Quebec-American antique trade and is amply illustrated with both black-and-white and color photographs, line drawings, and maps. An important reference work.
Size: 8 1/2" x 11"   254 photographs   160 pp.
Price Guide
ISBN:0-88740-276-3   softcover $24.95

Fine Wicker Furniture: 1870-1930 Tim Scott. The evolution of wicker furniture styles from 1870 to 1930 and preeminent manufacturers of the period are carefully explained with pertinent examples of their work illustrated in full color. A useful discussion of care and restoration of antique pieces is included. A wide variety of wicker furniture styles are highlighted, from ornate Victorian to Art Deco.
Size: 8 1/2" x 11"   330 photos   160 pp.
Price Guide
ISBN: 0-88740-231-3   soft cover $24.95

Furniture by Harrods Harrods Ltd. of London The 1905 furniture collection of Harrods displayed in exact photos and lithographs. Ranging from antique to modern styles, Harrods produced furniture for each room in the house, plus lighting devices, metal wares, cutlery, linens, porcelain, and glassware. Price guide included.
Size: 9" x 11"   8 pages in color   400 pp.
ISBN: 0-88740-180-5   soft cover $24.95

Furniture Made in America, 1875-1905 Richard and Eileen Dubrow. The Dubrows have exhaustively combined all original catalog material from major American furniture manufacturers of the 1880s and 90s enabling the reader to identify makers and give ideas of other pieces available—an especially important skill in light of the number of reproductions now appearing. Hundreds of examples including furniture for the dining room, parlours, library, bedroom and office are shown. A newly revised price guide makes this book a handy reference for all who are interested in furniture.
Size: 8 1/2" x 11"   Over 2000 illustrations 320 pp.
Price Guide
ISBN: 0-88740-695-5   soft cover $19.95

Golden Oak Furniture Velma Suzanne Warren. Over 670 color photographs, a descriptive text, and an extensive glossary of terms accompany examples of golden oak tables, chairs, sofas, sideboards, clocks, bedroom suites, chests, and cupboards of many varieties, organized by the room.
Size: 8 1/2" x 11"   674 color photos   160 pp.
Value Guide
ISBN: 0-88740-387-5   soft cover $29.95

Reupholstering at Home Peter Nesovich. Step-by-step instructions with 350 clear and detailed photographs show how to rebuild a dilapidated chair or sofa to look like new. Covered are the tools and materials you will need, and expert advice about which types of fabric are best for your needs. The author leads you through specific steps, with text, photographs, and captions to reupholster.
Size: 8 1/2" x 11"   176 pp.
ISBN: 0-88740-376-X   soft cover $14.95

Wallace Nutting, Supreme Edition, General Catalog. Wallace Nutting ran a successful business making reproductions with old-style techniques. This is the largest of his reproduction furniture catalogs from 1930, reprinted for today's collectors of old and Nutting furniture. The original 1930 price list is included.
Size: 6" x 9"   382 photos/drawings   160 pp.
ISBN: 0-916838-09-9   soft cover $10.95

American Furniture of the 19th Century, 1840-1880 Eileen and Richard Dubrow. This is an important study of the fine handcrafted furniture made in America from 1840 to 1880. Most pieces are identified by the cabinetmaker who made them, and biographies of the leading cabinetmakers from all over America are presented. There are special sections on Wooton desks and John Henry Belter.
Size: 8 1/2" x 11"   350 b/w photos   248 pp.
Index
ISBN: 0-916838-68-4   hard cover $30.00

American Furniture, Seventeenth, Eighteenth and Nineteenth Century Styles, Helen Comstock. In this classic volume, American furniture styles are presented historically. Craftsmen are described, their work is explained, and design innovations are shown. Chapters cover styles from Jacobean to Early Victorian.
Size: 8 1/2" x 11"   700 illustrations   336 pp.
ISBN: 0-916838-28-5   hard cover $44.95

Miniature Lamps Frank R. and Ruth E. Smith. The miniature glass oil and kerosene burning lamps were made in many variations in the 19th and early 20th centuries. The full-size lamps have been made continuously since 1825, when the originals were produced in Sandwich, Massachusetts, and these miniatures correspond in every detail with them. All of the component parts are explained thoroughly, and an extensive range of the variations is shown. 15 color plates
Size: 6 1/4" x 9 1/2"   630 b/w illustrations   285 pp.
ISBN: 0-916838-44-7   hard cover $29.95

American Lighting: 1840-1940 Nadja Maril. Using color photographs and rare catalog material from the American lighting industry, this is a welcome, valuable addition to the literature for historians, decorators, collectors, and others interested in the development of American design and technology.
Size: 9" x 12"   160 pp.
ISBN: 0-88740-879-6   hard cover $39.95

Nineteenth Century Lighting H. Parrott Bacot. A comprehensive study of candle-powered lighting devices from a period of just over 100 years that was witness to more inventions, developments, and improvements in lighting than during the entire previous history of man.
Size: 9" x 12"   394 b/w photos   240 pp.
ISBN: 0-88740-098-1   hard cover $59.95

Miniature Lamps II Ruth E. Smith. Almost 600 new examples and much historical material has been combined in this up-to-date study. The book illustrates a wide variety of lamps by many identified makers.
Size: 6 1/4" x 9 1/2"   595 photos   249 pp.
Index
ISBN: 0-916838-65-X   hard cover $28.50

Fairy Lamps, Elegance in Candle Lighting Bob & Pat Ruf. Over 800 lamps made from 1880 through the 1930s are shown in full color. The lamps range from the simplest examples given out with boxes of candles to the most extravagant chandelier assemblages made for lords, rajahs, and royalty. This work draws upon many primary sources to trace the development of fairy lamps, and catalogs examples that can be found on today's market.
Size: 8 1/2" x 11"   802 photos   240 pp.
Price Guide
ISBN 0-88740-975-X   hard cover $59.95

Miniature Victorian Lamps Marjorie Hulsebus. Miniature oil lamps are beautiful reminders of Victorian days, in glass, china, porcelain, brass, and silver. Styles range from the delicacy of the Victorian parlor through Art Nouveau elegance. This reference features almost 450 lamps never before seen in any book, with color photos and detailed information.
Size: 6" x 9"   Price Guide   192 pp.
ISBN: 0-88740-931-8   hard cover $39.95

Early Twentieth Century Lighting Sherwoods Ltd. of Birmingham. Sherwoods was one of the largest manufacturers of lighting devices in the early 20th century. Here are all forms of illumination devices then available for sale. Oil burning and electrically powered table and floor lamps, chandeliers, sconces, and lanterns are shown in vast numbers. Price guide.

Size: 9 3/4" x 12 1/4"	illustrated	200 pp.
ISBN: 0-88740-181-3	soft cover	$16.95

Pairpoint Lamps Edward and Sheila Malakoff. The complete range, diversity and beauty of these works of art from 1907 to 1929 are shown in this useful reference. More than 200 color photos, excerpts from company catalogs, and advertisements detail the designs, shade styles and sizes, and serial numbers of the lamps.

Size: 9" x 12"	Rarity Guide	160 pp.
ISBN: 0-88740-281-X	hard cover	$95.00

The Mirror Book: English, American, and European Herbert F. Schiffer. Large pictures of over 650 mirrors dating from Egyptian New Kingdom, circa 1300 B.C., through Art Nouveau at the beginning of the 20th century are arranged chronologically to show the development of styles plus information about the makers.

Size: 9" x 12"	704 photos	256 pp.
Index		
ISBN: 0-916838-82-X	hard cover	$45.00

20th Century Linens and Lace, A Guide to Identification, Care and Prices of Household Linens Elizabeth Scofield and Peggy Zalamea. The household linens and lace presented in this book are the collectible styles made in Europe and North America during the 20th century, including Appenzell, Battenberg, needle, bobbin, chemical and machine laces, crochet, cutwork, embroidery, damask, net darning, tatting and drawnwork. Beautiful color photographs depict the linens, from full room settings down to minute details of the stitches, and origin and quality are discussed.

Size: 8 1/2" X 11"	213 color photos	208pp.
Price Guide		
ISBN: 0-88740-826-5	hard cover	$39.95

Paperweights Sibylle Jargstorf. Hundreds of beautiful old and new paperweights are displayed in over 450 color photographs. This meticulously researched book presents a new historical view of international examples and their talented makers.

Size: 9" x 12"	455 photos	224 pp.
Value Guide		
ISBN: 0-88740-375-1	hard cover	$69.95

Collecting American Brilliant Cut Glass, 1876 - 1916 Bill and Louise Boggess. Cut glass of the 1876 to 1916 period with vital information collectors need to identify, select, and evaluate cut glass. Patterns are identified, signatures are shown, and major American companies are described. Thousands of cut glass pieces are shown in 1065 photographs. Each piece is graded for its rarity.

Size: 8 1/2" X 11"	1065 photos	320 pp.
Value Guide.		
ISBN: 0-88740-383-2	hard cover	$59.95

Identifying American Brilliant Cut Glass, Revised & Enlarged Edition. Bill and Louise Boggess. A basic reference and identification guide to use at auctions, shows, exhibits, and antique shops. It gives catalog names for various shapes and 280 patterns of American and Canadian glass. It presents 130 cut glass pieces known by their company signature, patent record or magazine ad. Over 800 exquisite photos.

Size: 6" x 9"	888 photos	284 pp.
Value Guide		
ISBN: 0-88740-296-8	soft cover	$19.95

Schiffer books may be ordered from your local bookstore, or they may be ordered directly from the publisher by writing to:
Schiffer Publishing, Ltd.
4880 Lower Valley Rd
Atglen PA 19310
(610) 593-1777; Fax (610) 593-2002
E-mail: schifferbk@aol.com
Please include $3.95 for shipping and handling for the first two books and 50¢ for each additional book. Free shipping for orders $100 or more.
Write for a free catalog.
Printed in USA